Architecture of Massively Parallel Microprocessor Systems

Patrick H. Stakem

Copyright (C) 1993, 2022

4th edition,

9th in Computer Architecture Series

Table of contents

3

Foreword

In the last 11 years, a lot has changed in this field. That's to be expected in a technology that is driven by Moore's Law, where complexity doubles every 18 months or so. So we have a factor of 7 or so, but actually the rate of change is increasing.

As I reviewed the existing material, I was struck by how many of the companies don't exist anymore.

Almost every one discussed. MPMS has essentially gone mainstream. I decided to leave the 1993 material essentially unchanged, tidied up a bit, removed some style and spelling errors. This becomes, then, a historical description on how the early days went.

Where we are today is machines built with multiple cores on one chip, each core being a complete computer. The same communication schemes discussed in this book are used, with the same trade-off's, shared memory or communication channel. We now have the technology to put many cores on one piece of silicon. Along the way, a parallel technology developed, that of graphics processing units. These are found in graphics interfaces to produce screen displays. There was a realization that general purpose computing could use these streamlined devices, and the community developed extensive code libraries for standard graphics cars. Now, multicore architectures are not necessarily ALU based; they contain multiple GPU's. There is a huge amount of computation available, compared to 11 years ago, but it is now chip-sized, not box-sized.

The same issues remain, and we have tackled the 1993-era difficult problems, and now face the 20014 much more difficult problems in computations. We don't seem to run out of difficult problems.

A very exciting project is the Beowulf cluster built from Raspberry-Pi modules by an individual, just because he could. The RaspberryPi is a deck-of-cards-sized computer board that can run linux. If you can run linux, you can run Beowulf. What we have is a 40 processor cluster in a standard pc tower case. It has 20 gigabytes of distributed ram, 5 terabytes of disk storage, and cost less than $3000.

If I am still around to upgrade this book again in 10 years, I expect this level of capability to be on my wrist, or implanted.

The physics hasn't changed, the technology is still pretty much the same, although improved, the software and communications principles are the same. No big breakthroughs here, just the relentless march of technology.

Foreword to the Third Edition

A table of contents was added, and some sections were updated with new material,

Foreward to the 4th edition

Well, the theory stands, but the implementations have changed. Just like mainframes are now our phone and tablets, and computing is not done on "big iron" but rather in the cloud, "massively parallel" now means cluster computers built from commodity ARM processor boards. Yes, Beowulf will still work.

Author

Mr. Stakem has an undergraduate degree in Electrical Engineering from Carnegie Mellon University, and Master's in Computer Science and Applied Physics from the Johns Hopkins University.

He taught for the Johns Hopkins University, Loyola University in Maryland, and Capitol Technology University. He spent 42 years supporting projects at all of the NASA Centers. He has a particular fascination with technology.

Mr. Stakem may be found on Facebook and Linkedin.

Acknowledgments

These pages would not have happened without the support and contributions of the following people and organizations, and others that I have forgotten: Deb Richmond, Ray Lloyd, Jeff Wilson, Marco Figueiredo, Dr. Tushar Hazra, Chuck Ashton, IBM Corp., Inmos Corp., Texas Instruments, Motorola, Intel, Ross Technologies, HP, Transtech Parallel Systems, Meiko, Mercury Computer Systems, Sky Computers, nCube, Tera Computer, MasPar, Pyramid, Cray Computers, NEC, Kendell Square Research, Convex Computer, Parsytec, Thinking Machines Corp., Tandem Computers, Northbridge Computer, and others.

Background

By the 1990's, it was becoming increasingly obvious that Massively Parallel Microprocessor-based Systems (MPMS) were becoming significant new forces in the marketplace, as well as a design approach of great importance.

There is no one good source that discusses the architecture of MPMS. No one text gives the overall view of MPMS as a design philosophy, as a market force, and as a technology driver. Thus, I took on the thankless task of putting together this set of information. It is important to realize that in a rapidly moving, trendy area such as MPMS, by the time information is published, it is probably obsolete. By the time a book is published, it is probably only of historical significance. Thus, a set of web pages gives a timely set of information.

This set of pages is intended for the hardware or software practitioner to use as an introduction to the subject. It assumes that the reader know something about the internals of computer systems, architecture, and instruction execution. It would be relevant for an advanced undergraduate or graduate level course in computer design or architecture. It discusses the chip level of MPMS, and looks at the design trade-offs at the systems level.

Because systems without feedback are not stable, I actively solicit feedback from users and readers of this book. If you use it in a course, or for background information, let me know what I did wrong, what I did not include, and where the mistakes are.

Scope

This document covers the field of MPMS. This is a subset of the field of Massively Parallel Computers. Although this variety of computer has been around for a long time, it only started to make an impact on the computer industry in the 1990's, as an alternative to supercomputers.

The goal of this document is to give the reader an

introductory look at the fundamentals of MPMS design, to allow the reader to understand the trade-offs, limitations, speed, cost, complexity, and architectures. The reader will be shown the history and the trends of the technology of this rapidly moving field. To achieve these goals, we'll review the basics and background of the technology, to understand where the trade-offs are. We'll then look at real-world design examples to see how the trade-offs were made. It is essential to realize that in MPMS technology, as in many cutting edge endeavors, there are no wrong answers in the marketplace, but a multitude of right ones. The wrong answers either never make it to the market, or don't last long there.

This is not a source for designers, because the level of detail presented is not sufficient. However, it will be useful for engineers and engineering managers that must make use of this technology in systems. They need to know the capabilities and limitations of this important field, to be able to apply the technology in their particular domains of expertise.

MPMS is a rapidly evolving field. Software has not begun to catch up with the processors. Good software tools to develop, debug, and maintain MPMS are just emerging.

In many cases we'll see decisions made that were not influenced totally by the technological issues, but mainly by marketing considerations. To the design engineer, this is heresy, but in the cold, cruel world, this is economic survival. Some companies are the pioneers at the "bleeding edge" of technology development; others prefer to hold back and address mature markets. As Nolan Bushnell says, "The Pioneers are the ones with the arrows in them".

How these pages are organized

The first three sections introduce the definitions of MPMS technology, and give an historical context. We will place the MPMS paradigm within the general field of computer architecture and design, and specifically, parallel computers. We'll define the relevant terms. Then we discuss the important issue of software development tools for parallel systems. After that, the next section presents details on the chip level products used as a basis for the processing portion of these systems. We discuss the critical issues of communications between system elements. The next section discusses the ancillary issues of memory, including disk and tape storage for large systems. The next section presents a series of architectural design examples of systems, both historical and current. Manufactures contact information, is included. A glossary of terms and definitions is given. A bibliography is included, including books, relevant articles, and key papers.

The first section presents the background, scope and organization of these pages, and discusses some of the history of the technology. It presents metrics we can apply to parallel systems, and discusses some of the limitations of the basis technology. In the next section, we'll present the basics of MPMS. We need to review the building block elements of a computer. Then, the next section presents the MPMS approaches to high performance computing, first by identifying the bottlenecks, and showing how each of these are addressed.

We then examine the software tools to develop, debug, and maintain parallel systems. In essence, software makes or breaks the MPMS approach (as some companies have painfully learned), because software enables us to harness the raw throughput of the hardware to do useful work.

We are now ready to see how real-world companies have approached microprocessors. Although in theory one could build a parallel machine with almost any processor, some lend themselves better to parallelization. We'll examine the leading contenders, and examine what differentiates them from ordinary machines. The choice for system designers is a cheap, commodity processor, or a custom processor, which specific features for parallelism. We'll explore both approaches. We discuss the various critical approaches to interconnection of elements. We then balance the discussion of processing with that of mass storage systems. In the next section, we'll examine how these processor chips are integrated into board and system level products to construct MPMS machines that rival and exceed supercomputers at a fraction of the cost.

Use of this book

This section discusses the suggested uses of these pages for several audiences. These pages are intended as an introduction to the MPMS architecture, and as a reference for practicing Information Technology Systems professionals. They are addressed to system level designers and architects, and information professionals who are planning and implementing strategic business systems built around this technology. There is a glossary of terms, jargon, and abbreviations.

For the Working Professional

These pages are written at the advanced undergraduate or graduate engineering level. Practicing Information Technology Professionals, engineers, system architects, and software designers will be able to use them directly. Technical Management and Technical Sales will also find them of use. Commodity RISC chips are the basis for engineering workstations and large, massively parallel machines. RISC processors are the technology engines that form the basis for the current and emerging generation of MPMS system. Unix is the software system of choice, and c/c++ is the language. Other contenders seek to attain critical mass. MPMS systems based on RISC chips are challenging traditional large mainframe systems for the lead in supplying mips to enterprises. This is a technology that has to be monitored, and the advances occur rapidly. The professional or the student will learn:

- who are the key players?
- what are the key architectural features?
- what are the strengths and weaknesses of the technology, and what are its limitations?
- where did the basis technology come from, and where is it going?

The various company technical representatives and technical sales people I have spoken with have universally praised the concept of these pages. Their view is that they have a very narrow focus on their own product, and no good mechanism to see what the competition is doing, or to provide compare-and-contrast information. Sales representatives, even though they may not have a technical background, understand the jargon.

Use in a Course

These pages can serve as the text for a course in MPMS computer architecture, or as a supplemental text for a more general computer architecture course. The first four sections present the introduction to the subject, and the student should be intimately familiar with this material before proceeding. I assume that the student is familiar with the industry jargon, but a glossary is included. The basic assumption is that the student understands how an instruction is executed, but this is reviewed. I recommend reading the sections consecutively starting from the beginning, slowing down as necessary. For use as a reference, the reader may proceed directly to the detailed chip discussions and system descriptions.

The technical material in these pages is not as detailed as that available from the manufacturers, but these pages do abstract over 100 different vendor data books and presentations. Material from significant architectures is included, even if that architecture is no longer offered in the marketplace. I would be interested in hearing how these pages are applied.

MPMS basics

This chapter examines the basics of the MPMS design philosophy. First, we need to reexamine the history of the underlying technology.

Current computer architectures evolved from machines designed when memory was an expensive resource. Instruction sets were encoded to reduce memory usage. Unfortunately, these instructions are time consuming to decode. Coupled with multiple addressing modes that may involve multiple accesses of memory to resolve the final operand address, the decoding of these complex instructions presented a major bottleneck. The same technological limits to memory complexity limited the amount of silicon dedicated to instruction decoding, forcing microprogramming, or decoding using look-up tables and microsteps.

The fetch/execute cycle

To understand MPMS computers, we must understand how computers operate . In this section, we will review the elements of a computer, the fetch/execute cycle, and how instructions are executed.

Any computer can be thought of as having three main elements or building blocks. These are the Processing Element (PE), the memory, and the Input/Output section. The processing element handles the mathematical and logical operations on data, and the flow of control. The memory, which is probably organized hierarchically, holds the data and instructions. The I/O section allows for the user interface, and provides a communication path to other systems or devices.

It is important to remember that processor and memory speeds are not always well matched. At the current time, processors are much faster than affordable memory.

Memories are dense, regular silicon structures. Processors are dense, not very regular structures. Processors tend to be regular along the word size, but memories are millions of the same cell design, replicated to the limits of manufacturing technology. Memory production lends itself to economy of scale much more so than processors.

The actual fetch/execute cycle is broken down into several micro cycles. We will define the basic micro phases to be:

    1) opcode fetch (memory read)
    2) instruction decode (cpu)
    3) Operand fetch (if applicable) (memory read)

4) instruction execution (cpu)
5) update program counter (cpu)
6) operand write (if applicable) (cpu)

We will define each of these steps to take one clock cycle. Now, an obvious way to speed up the whole fetch/execute process is to overlap each of the above steps. In essence, we assign a sub-PE to each step, and let these 6 units do 6 things collectively in one clock cycle. But, the above steps are not independent. For example, we can't do step 2 until step 1 is complete. We can't really do step 5 until step 4 is complete, in case we have a branch or jump instruction. Step 3 and 6 may not even be present. What is the solution? We pipeline or assembly-line process the sub-steps. This introduces a latency, because of the pipeline depth. Pipelining will be discussed in detail later.

MPMS Architectures

This section will discuss the architectural approaches in using large numbers of microprocessors connected together into one machine. Although most entrants in this arena choose to take advantage of the economies of scale of merchant RISC chips, some choose to design their own. Notable among the latter are KSR and nCube. The rationale for the custom design is that the additional "glue" logic required around the off-the-shelf chip to allow it to be integrated into a system provides a level of complication at the system level. Single chip MPMS nodes such as nCube's allow for extremely simple, and thus inexpensive nodes. The correct approach is not obvious, and, as in many cases, it may turn out that there are several correct answers. The success or failure of competing approaches depend on a myriad of factors, some technical, some financial, some marketing. We will address all of the approaches in subsequent sections.

Interconnection of Elements

In this section, we address architectural approaches to coordinating the use of multiple processors. Most of these approaches will work with any underlying technology, and are useful after the maximum speed of a single processor in a given technology has been wrung out.

One approach to solving increasing complex problems with increasingly capable hardware is simply to wait. Given enough time, sufficiently complex hardware for the problem domain will emerge. However, it is increasingly apparent that software development lags hardware to the extent that software tools do not emerge until the hardware is obsolete by at least two generations. Also, the capabilities of any given hardware design will be exceeded by computational problems of interest well into the foreseeable future. At any given point of technological complexity, a cluster of coordinated processors can outperform a single processor. Thus, faced with a seemingly inexhaustible complex problem domain, along with industry emphasis on hardware development, we need to tackle both the software and the communication domains to better utilize the hardware available at any given point. Software will be discussed in section 4. Here, we want to discuss the critical issue of communications among elements.

The bottleneck to getting more than one processor to work on a given problem domain at one time is the communications. There is an upper bound in a bus-oriented, shared memory SMP systems, arising from the communication limit of the bus interconnect (a classic Shannon channel limit). Clusters of computers also suffer from an interprocessor communication limit, from the LAN-like interconnect. Some MPP's are like clusters in a box.

Shared memory MPP's usually do not have a homogeneous communication environment, due to communication bandwidth restrictions. A two tier communications architecture is used, with shared memory intrabox, and a lan type point-point link for interbox messaging. Since MPP machines have to scale to thousands of processors, a distributed memory scheme is usually chosen. Another approach is to cluster SMP's. Data sharing is the key, and the critical issue for large parallel relational database applications. The performance will be made (or broken) by the sophistication of the interconnection scheme. Speed and latency are of critical importance. Latency predominates for short messages.

Consider the case of having to send a large volume of data from New York to California. We look at two options: we rent a gigabit class line, and transfer the data serially at OC-48, or about 2.4 gigabits per second. The latency, from the time a bit enters the line at New York until it exits at California, is very short, and depends on the time it takes light to traverse 2000 miles of cable. This is an expensive option. We could also decide to charter a 747 freighter, and load it with floppy disks. Here, the latency is about 5 hours, but the data all arrives together. One case emphasizes speed, the other case emphasizes low latency.

Again, let's look at an analogy. If we want to get across town using the bus system, we wait at the bus stop for the next available bus. The wait time is our latency, and is random, depending on when we arrive with respect to the bus's arrival. If we go only a few blocks, the latency may be commensurate with or even exceed the travel time. If we go across country on the bus, the latency is totally dominated by the travel time. Even in town, if we need to change buses, we introduce another latency between getting dropped off by bus-1 and picked up by bus-2. We may need to cross town in several of these 'hops', each with its own latency. For one person, this may not be efficient. For large aggregates of people, it makes sense.

Alternately, we can call a cab, and go directly from where we are to our destination. There is still a wait-latency, but the travel time is reduced, and the cost is higher. The best case, the fastest travel time, is that we jump into a worm-hole that connects directly where we want to go. Then, the hole closes up behind us.

In the interconnect hierarchy, the node-node connection is frequently made via shared memory. Thus, a node may be an SMP architecture in its own right, with two or four processor elements. this approach does not scale well beyond about 16 processors. The node-node communication is tightly coupled.

Between nodes, a loosely coupled message passing scheme is usually employed. This uses a LAN-like architecture that can take one of many topological forms. Popular are the mesh, torus, hypercube, and tree. The following table shows the approaches taken by some of the major vendors.

Interconnect Topology of some MIMD machines

Company	Machine	interconnect
Cray	T3D	3D torus
KSR	KSR-2	toroid
TMC	CM-5	fat tree
Convex	Exemplar	torus
Intel SSD	Paragon	2D mesh
nCube	nCube-3	hypercube
Tandem	K10K	torus
Meiko	CS-2	fat tree

Intel favors the mesh architecture for their Paragon series, based on work done at CalTech. The chip instantiation is the iMRC (mesh router component). This allows vendors to interconnect chips such as the i860 and Pentium.

The early iPSC series uses as many as one-hundred twenty-eight 40-mhz i860xr chips. Special I/O nodes used a shared I/O design are based on the i80386. The internal networked, called 'Direct-Connect', provided bidirectional 5.6 Mbyte/second channels in a switched configuration. The Paragon machine scales to 1024 of the i860XP processors, arranged in SMP type, 4 processor nodes. Each node can have up to 128 Mbytes of memory. The interprocessor communication architecture scales as nodes are added. A 2D mesh configuration, with a mesh router for each node, provides a message passing architecture with a bi-directional node-node bandwidth of 200 Mbytes per second, and a latency of 40 Nanoseconds per node hop.

Intel's Paragon machine scales to 1024 of the 50 Mhz. i860XP processors, arranged in SMP-type, 4 processor nodes. Each node can have up to 128 mbytes of memory. The nodes are interconnected in a mesh. Future Paragon models will incorporate the Pentium chip or subsequent, and development on the 64 bit successor to the i860 will be (or has been) dropped. The "Touchstone Delta" System is a one of a kind system built for the California Institute of Technology using 520 of the i860 chips.

NCube, the Intel iWarp, and the Transputer use the hypercube architecture. In each case, the basic processor chip has a communications capability built in. The Transputer and the iWarp have 4 high speed serial nodes each, and the nCube chip has 12, going to 16 for the nCube3. This allows a direct connection to each nearest neighbor in n-space. Thus, the Transputer and iWarp can each be directly connected in an Order-4 hypercube, and the nCube2 in an order 12.

The iWarp achieves a communication to computation ratio of 1:1. Each iWarp component consists of an integer and a floating point computation section, and a communication element. The communication element supports 4 full duplex I/O channels, of 160 Mbytes/second input and output capability. Message passing exploits worm-hole routing for low overhead. Multiple logical connections on one physical channel is possible, similar to Inmos' virtual link concept. Fine grained, systolic communication is supported.

A crossbar switch may be used if the processor does not support sufficient interconnects. The Inmos C004 16x16 crossbar switch chip provides this function for the serial links of the Transputer. A crossbar switch functions like a telephone company central office, connecting any input to any output upon demand. The circuit remains for the duration of the message, or can be quasi-permanent. The latency introduced by the switch is minimal, about 1/2 bit time in the Inmos case. This is important where several switches must be traversed.

The nCube' machine's interconnection is via a hypercube topology. Each nCube2 has 13 I/O engines, one of which is used for I/O. Thus, an order 12 Hypercube is supported, or up to 4096 nodes. The worst case (longest distance) communication latency is on the order of the

Hypercube, or 12, in the largest configuration. The nCube3 machine will use a new chip that will operate at 50 Mhz. Up to 65k processors can be included, since each processor chip includes 18 channels, 16 for the hypercube, and 2 for I/O. The channels now operate at 100mbps, due to use of 2 bit parallel (up from 1 bit, serial). nCubes's differentiater is its interconnection speed, at 2.5 megabytes/second bi-directional, with a factor of 10 improvement coming. The nCube-III will have dynamic routing, where each channel can support transfers at 20 Mbytes/second. There will be 18 communications channels on-chip, each 4 bits wide (2 in, 2 out). The channels will operate at 2x clock, 50 mbytes/second peak each, or 200 mbytes/second aggregate. The latency will be less than 2 microseconds, with 200 nanosecond internode forwarding. Adaptive routing will be used.

This architecture uses a 'FAT TREE' interconnect, favored by Meiko and Thinking Machines for the CM-5 series. A key factor is whether the tree is 'pruned' or complete. What differentiates the CS-2 from the TMC CM-5 is that the CS-2 uses a complete tree interconnect, where the CM-5 uses a pruned tree. In theory, the CS-2 has a larger bi-sectional bandwidth as the system scales to larger numbers of nodes. The Meiko architecture supports up to 8 layers in the tree, giving a worst case path in a 256 node configuration of 7 switches. The maximum delay thru a tree architecture is on the order of the tree. Meiko's bi-sectional bandwidth scales to 102 Gbytes /second. There is an independent low bandwidth parallel bus for diagnostics and maintenance.

The inter-processor communications topology and chips are of Meiko's design. The Elan and ELITE chip are made by Texas Instruments. The ELAN is the network interface processor on each compute node. It provides a coherent Mbus processor interface. The ELITE is the network switch processor, which is a 4x4 full crossbar. The ELITE achieves a 10 microsecond latency with a linear (scalable) bisection bandwidth. What differentiates the CS-2 from the TMC CM-5 is that the CS-2 uses a complete tree interconnect, where the CM-5 uses a pruned tree. In theory, the CS-2 has a larger bisectional bandwidth as the system scales to larger numbers of nodes. The Meiko architecture supports up to eight layers in the tree, giving a worst case path in a 256 node configuration of 7 switches.

Each I/O connection of TMC's fat-tree interconnect provides a 20 Mbyte/second bisection bandwidth, that scales. Latency ranges from 3-7 microseconds. A separate control network is maintained, that supports broadcast and combining functions, and global synchronization. A diagnostic network uses JTAG and a special software diagnostics package. The TM-5 machine is scalable to 16,000 units.

The Torus arrangement is a 3-D structure, used by Tandem, Convex, and the Cray T3D. The T3d is scalable to hundreds or thousands of processors, using its sophisticated interconnect and memory system. It can support up to 2048 compute nodes, using a 3-D torus interconnection. The interconnect is bi-directional 2 bytes wide, and gives a peak transfer rate of 300 Mbps between nodes. The sustained bandwidth is about half that. Transfers are directed, and packet switched. The T3D implements Cray's shared distributed memory scheme, in which any processor can address any memory in the system. The base Alpha processor's data translation lookaside buffer (D-TLB) has been extended to resolve memory address to the node where it resides. Each node hosts up to 64 Mbytes. A random read anywhere in the Torus interconnect can be satisfied within 1 microsecond.

The Convex Exemplar supports up to 128 processors, organized as hypernodes of up to 8 processors connected by a crossbar, of bandwidth 2.5 gigabytes/second. Interconnect latency is on the order of 100's of nanoseconds. Each hypernode has its own memory that is shared among the processors in the hypernode. A hypernode can be thought of as a tightly coupled, shared memory SMP. I/O interfaces are distributed across the hypernodes. A second level torroidal interconnect is used between hypernodes. This scalable torroidal interconnect (sci) is based on the IEEE Scalable Coherent Interface (IEEE 1596-1992), and provides 4 unidirectional rings with a capacity of up to 2 gigabytes per second. Sequential access to memory are interleaved across the rings of the toroid, for load balancing. The hypernode can be thought as a tightly coupled, fine-grained system, and the collection of hypernodes can be thought of as a coarse-grained, message-passing architecture. The overall machine has coherent distributed memory, and a large I/O system that is also distributed. Sixty four channels per I/O unit can be used, to a total of 4096 channels. The Service processor functionality is distributed among the hypernodes, with options for boot, diagnostics, and monitoring. JTAG is used for diagnostic scans of the hardware. A systems console (service hypernode) is used, with a separate and independent DaRT (diagnostic and testing bus), that operates in parallel with the interconnect busses.

Networking between nodes in the Tandem system takes one of several forms. For up to 16 cpu's, 4 gigabytes of memory, and 64 I/O channels, a TorusNet internal networking architecture is used. For up to 224 cpu's, 57 gigabytes of memory, and 896 I/O channels, a variation called the TorusNet Domain is used. For the high end system, the multi-domain TorusNet supports 4080 cpu's.
Shared Memory Systems

If we have 2 or 4 processors, we may connect these with a multiported memory. The memory would include the contention resolution mechanisms to arbitrate between processors attempting to access a single location simultaneously.

The problem with this approach is that multiported memory (MPM) is expensive, of small capacity, and does not scale well beyond about 4 ports. This approach, however, has some merit, particularly if the processors and MPM can be combined onto one chip, or multichip module.

The next approach would be to have a very fast bus connecting processors with large caches. In fact, we could consider the memory as totally consisting of cache. This is KSR's approach.

In the KSR design, all of memory is treated as cache. A Harvard style, separate bus for instruction and memory is used. Each node board contains 256kbytes of I-cache and D-cache, essentially primary cache. At each node is 32 megabytes of memory for main cache. The system level architecture is shared virtual memory, which is physically distributed in the machine. The programmer or application only sees one contiguous address space, which is spanned by a 40 bit address. Traffic between nodes travels at up to 4 gigabytes per second. The 32 Megabytes per node, in aggregate, forms the physical memory of the machine.

KSR uses a ring architecture with 32 processors per ring on the KSR1, 64 processors in the KSR2. Scalability is achieved by interconnecting multiple rings via a hierarchical fat tree. KSR implements a ring topology (toroidal). This topology has some interesting features. By coupling two rings by a high-speed WAN, systems could be geographically distributed but still appear to be a single computer.

Distributed Memory Systems

Looking at the communication problem from another angle, we may decide to tackle it not from a memory but from an I/O standpoint. In the distributed memory approach, we have a processor and memory at each node, and a communications network connects these nodes. Again, several options present themselves. We can use dedicated, point-point links. This scheme is limited in scalability by the number of links available, and the interfacing hardware. For example, the Transputer chip comes with 4 dedicated I/O links, each capable of 20 mbps per second each. At the node end, the links terminate in a dma engine that interfaces with the processor's memory. In the case of the Transputer, all of this is on one chip. Similarly, the proprietary chip used by nCube in their latest machine has 16 links for interprocessor communication. The iWarp chip has 4 channels, and the TMS series of RISC-DSP chips has 6. Most of these links are asynchronous serial, but the TI chip has parallel links, limiting the distance between processors. On the other hand, the parallel scheme is faster, and particularly if you plan to pull it all onto one chip, as TI did with their TMS320C080 variant.

Distributed memory systems come with a "built-in" physical communication scheme between processors. On top of this, we need a communications and messaging protocol, interfaced with the operating system. One approach is the public domain software package PVM (Parallel Virtual Machine).

Speaking of operating systems, we can choose to implement the entire operating system at each node of the distributed memory system, but this uses up a lot of memory, particularly for Unix. Another approach is to have a kernel at each node, requiring several hundred kbytes, as opposed to 10's of Megabytes. Support for parallel distributed systems is emerging in several operating systems, notably for Windows-NT and OS-2.

In the distributed memory model, there is no requirement to have homogeneous systems. The distributed system resembles a network or a cluster of minicomputers more than one big homogeneous machine. Software such as PVM can link diverse systems across the communications network into one large worker.

MPMS characteristics in review

In Summary, we can list the characteristics of MPMS machines that we will examine in detail starting in the next chapter. Not all examples will share all of the characteristics, and most will violate some.

Taxonomy of Systems

This section strives to put MPMS machines in categories and classifications.

The classical taxonomy in computer systems is credited to Michael Flynn:. SISD, SIMD, MISD,MIMD

Flynn's taxonomy:

SISD	Single instruction, single data uniprocessor
SIMD	Single instruction, multiple data uniprocessor with time-multiplexed data streams, or multiprocessors running the same program; examples NASA MPP, Connection Machine, array processors
MISD	Multiple Instruction, single data multiprocessor with one data stream
MIMD	Multiple instruction, multiple data Multiprocessor, multiple programs, multiple data streams

A processing metric for throughput is typically given in mips and m-flops. This may actually represent best case, guaranteed not-to-exceed no-ops per second. I/O throughput is typically given in bytes /second. Storage is characterized by bytes, or, perhaps, bytes per unit volume. Of equal concern is volatility.

For processor:I/O balance, we can use mips per megabyte per second, similar to Kung's Alpha parameter. This simplifies to operations/byte, representing operations on every byte of throughput data. In signal processing capabilities, a number of 3-10 is typical. In computation environments such as statistics, a number like 10-100 is typical. At the other end of the spectrum, in data intensive environments, a number like 0.1 to 0.001 is more typical. The achievable Alpha depends heavily on whether a distributed or a shared memory architecture is used.

Metrics

We need some way to compare systems, and what is usually considered is operations per second. This has lead to blatant misuses, and benchmarkmanship among companies, and confusion among users and potential buyers. What we want is to compare apples to apples, but all we have is a fruit salad. Rumors abound of machine architectures optimized for particular industry benchmarks. In addition, because there is no generic parallel architecture, industry standard benchmarks are difficult to arrive at. Raw mips or megaflops is one measure of performance, and the processor:I/O balance is another.

Limits

One area to explore is the limits to the performance of the technology. Since the thrust of the MPMS ideology is the quest for speed of computation, it is informative to explore what limits are imposed on this parameter, and where these limits derive from.

Technology has begun to hit the fundamental physical limitations in hardware development. These include the speed of light as an upper limit to communication speed and the uncertainty principle as a lower limit to feature size in storage and processing media. In the near term, hardware capability will continue to develop at an increasingly rapid rate, but will begin to decrease in complexity rate without fundamental breakthroughs. In particular, processor capability will outstrip the ability to provide fast memory access, sufficiently fast I/O, or to develop code. One solution is to develop methodologies for applying multiple processors in parallel to large and complex problem sets of interest. This approach is applicable at any point in the technology curve. Moore's Law presents the empirical observation that chip complexity has doubled and is doubling roughly every 18 months. Obviously, this can't continue forever. But, it is continuing, but at considerable cost.

What are the limits to the basis technology? The answer to this question sets limits on sequential processors. The speed of light is roughly 12 inches per nanosecond in vacuum, and slower than that in other media. The mobility of charge carriers in silicon GaAs or other semiconductors is significantly less than the speed of light. Similarly, we need to consider the fabrication technology. What is the limit of resolution of visible light, x-rays, e-beams, etc. This is currently below one micron, and busing 0.1 micron. One factor that is working in our favor is that, as devices get smaller, and features get closer together, communication times drop, and operating speed rises. At the same time, power density goes up, and devices are in danger of melting from their own operation. This is a driver for the recent push from the traditional 5 volt devices to 3.3 and lower voltages, as the power goes as the square of the voltage. Another factor is the ability to distinguish levels and sense transitions. The binary system uses two levels, and we must be able to distinguish between them for system operations.

There are several key questions to consider in assessing this technology. These are presented without answers, to provide a basis for further thought:

- Is there a practical upper limit to processing speed? And, are we nearing that limit?
- Is there an upper limit to memory size? Thirty-two bits of addressing used to be thought sufficient, but recently the trend is towards 64 bits. How many are really needed?
- Is there an upper limit to connectivity or I/O speed? What do we have to communicate with, and at what speed? What latency is acceptable?
- What are the requirements for "intelligent" systems? What level of processing is required for systems for vision, human level processing, dolphin level sonar, etc.
- where are the computational barriers that prevent or limit progress in the physical and biological sciences?

The heart of MPMS is derived from what is termed "Flynn's anomaly", which basically states that, at best, a processor element (PE) can only do one thing per clock cycle. One solution is to speed up the clock rate, so we get more clock cycles per unit time. This areas simply goes with the flow in modern digital design, where basic system clock rate has been increasing according to

Moore's law since chips were first made. Another approach is to have multiple processor elements, each doing one thing per clock cycle. This results in a parallel or vector machine, the MISD or MIMD of Flynn's taxonomy. Several architectures lend themselves particularity well to this approach.

Processor-I/O Balance and scalability

Any given data processing architecture will have bottlenecks, because either the processor is waiting for the memory (processor stall), or the memory is waiting for the processor (I/O bound). Communications speed is limited by the minimum channel capacity in the system, and processing speed is limited by the slowest hardware element. Ideally, the computation rate should balance the I/O rate, but this is a function of the problem domain, and the algorithm. Some data can be buffered in memory, but onboard memory is an expensive resource.

For example, the combination of four serial links of one Transputer together can transmit a total of about 1 million 32 bit words per second, both in and out simultaneously. If the on-chip ram is used primarily for instructions, and most data is flowed through the data links, then for each new word of data, 10 instructions can be executed. The on-chip 4k can hold a significant amount of code for the RISC Architecture and the data links can in theory supply new data fast enough for even the shortest algorithms and tightest loops. In other words, the data handling and computational speeds seem to be well matched. The data can be supplied by either the results of prior processes or by transputers used for data routing . The data routers will each have expanded external memories and can be thought of as servers for large blocks of shared data. The data routers will serve as very smart gate keepers of that data for the main processing engine. They can also be used as system masters to hold and execute large blocks of less time critical code for high level control of computational resources. They might even swap time critical code in and out of the main engine in real time as tasks change.

If 10% of the code consumes 90% of the time which is a commonly assumed ratio, then a well balanced system would consist of multiple transputers to run time critical code with data routers able to support caching of less frequently used code, to control system overall dataflow, and to provide redundancy.

Looking at how a typical executing program might be balanced in this system, assume five identical processes being executed in parallel. Data routing transputers send a 32 bit data word to one instrument Transputer. These instrument Transputer execute 10 instructions then pass a 32 bit result on to another instrument Transputer which execute 10 instructions and so on down a string of 20 transputers (200 instructions executed total) and the result is sent back to the data routers. So long as at least 200 instructions need to be executed for each new word of data, the instrument transputers are not starved for data. Clearly, this is an idealized example and no parallel processor can be 100% efficient in using instruction cycles. The point is that this architecture is within the range of a reasonable data-flow-to-processing ratio.

Operations/byte - several processors

Note that the metric of interest, ops/byte is to be maximized, as this represents the number of operations that can be performed on each byte of incoming data at maximum data flow rate.

Examining the general computational problem domain including the full spectrum from matrix multiplication (compute-bound) to matrix addition (I/O bound) is seen. Compute bound processes can always be speeded up by faster computational components, faster memory, or a smarter architecture. I/O bound problems present a greater challenge. In fact, it is relatively easy to transform a compute bound problem to an I/O bound problem with a parallel processor. One solution, studied at Carnegie-Mellon University, is the systolic processor, which is a matrix of simple, interconnected processor elements with I/O at the boundaries, and a pipelined processing approach to data that is pulsed through the array. In this scheme (since instantiated in the iWarp product, by Intel), multiple use can be made of each data item, and a high throughput can be achieved with modest I/O rate. There is extensive concurrency and modular expand-ability, and the control and data flow are simple and regular. This technique, easily implemented on transputers, lends itself well to repetitive operations on large data sets, such as those generated by spaceborne sensors.

Scalable systems, those made up of multiple computational & communication building blocks, have an architecture that is responsive to the problem domain. In such a homogeneous system, the correct amount of processing and I/O can be provided for the initial requirements, with the ability to expand later in a building block fashion to address evolved requirements as well as redundancy or fault tolerance. Developing software for scale-able systems is a challenge, mostly in deciding how the software is spread across the computational nodes. This is a solvable problem, based both on good software tools and on programmer experience. Research into these topics as well as the ability of the system itself to adapt to processing load, is ongoing. Transputer networks, discussed in chapter seven, use modular building blocks with integral communication capabilities to build networks that can offer linear problem speedup. This is obvious with compute-intensive, minimal communication tasks such as the Mandelbrot set, which could ideally use one processor element per pixel to calculate the image. Each point in the Mandelbrot set is independent of its neighbors. If we run a particular instance of the Mandelbrot set on a single Transputer, then multiple units, and graph the run times against the number of processor elements, we will see a near-linear speedup. In the general case this is true, until the problem becomes more communication bound than compute bound. As a "best case", the Mandelbrot is an ideal benchmark; completely computationally intensive.

Of course, the applicability of the parallel processor to a given problem set implies that the applicable algorithm can be parallelized, and a solution can be implemented and debugged in a reasonable time. This implies that an efficient programming and debugging environment exist for the selected hardware. This is certainly the case for Transputer-based systems. The major hurdle is conceptual for the systems integraters - the ability to think in parallel paradigms. This comes with hands-on experience.

Thought Questions for this section:

- What are the key features of parallel computers versus uni-processors?
- What limits the ability to collect uniprocessors into multiprocessor systems
- What are the relative costs of latency versus limited bandwidth in interconnection of processor elements?

Commodity chip level products

This section provides a look at the technical details of some of the chips used as a basis for the construction of the various parallel machines.

This section discusses the main commodity chip-level processor products that lend themselves to being paralleled. Although in theory any microprocessor can be used in that mode, some are much better at it than others. The system level designers choice is between a merchant RISC chip, or a custom chip. This section discusses the applicable merchant chips available. Proprietary and custom chips are discussed with the relevant machine architecture in a later section.

The following chart shows the processor (this chapter) usage by system vendor.

Processor Usage by System Vendor

- Proprietary
    KSR, Maspar, nCube
- HP-PA
    HP, Convex
- SPARC
    TM, Meiko, Cray SuperServer
- Alpha
    DEC, Cray T3D/T3E
- MIPS

NEC, CDC
- PowerPC
  IBM (SP-1, SP-2), Parsytech
- Pentium, PentiumPro
  Intel SSD, NCR, Unisys, Sequent, Pyramid
- Transputer T-800, T-9000
  Transtech, Meiko
- iWarp
  Intel
- i860
  Intel SSD, Cray, Transtech, Meiko

iWARP

The iWarp is a VLSI instantiation of Kung's work on a parallel architecture in progress for many years, referred to as Warp, and at Carnegie Mellon University on the earlier CMMP and CM* projects. Resembling the Transputer, the iWarp is a processor and memory unit that is hooked into networks of communication channels among processor elements. The original architecture for systolic computing arrays grew out of DARPA's interest in and support via the Strategic Computing Program. The Warp architecture exhibits fine grain parallelism, in the sense of few calculations per I/O.

The goal of the iWarp program was to develop a compute/communicate architecture that would scale in both dimensions. Message passing would exploit worm-hole routing for low overhead. Multiple logical connections on one physical channel would be possible,

41

similar to Inmos' virtual link concept. Fine grained, systolic communication would be supported. The iWarp would be RISC-like in having a one instruction per clock, with a very long instruction (VLIW) architecture. The iWarp designers strove to achieve a balance between communication and computation, which would address problems spanning the range from fine-grained to coarse grained. In addition, they wanted state of the art vector and scalar performance. Zero overhead communication, like the Transputer's links, was desired.

The architecture is systolic, in the sense that data is pumped in "waves" throughout the processor system, much in the same way that the heart's systolic rhythm pumps blood throughout the body. iWarp is used to build scalable parallel processors.

The iWarp achieves a communication to computation ratio of 1:1. Each iWarp component consists of an integer and a floating point computation section, and a communication element. The communication element supports 4 full duplex I/O channels, of 160 Mbytes/second input and output capability. The computation element supports 20 mips of integer operations, and 20 mFlops of (single precision) floating point performance. The memory access of the computation element supports 160 mbytes/second.

The integer execution unit has an 8k rom for initialization and self test. The floating point unit includes an adder and multiplier that can operate in parallel. DMA support is provided. An event pin is used for interrupts. A timer is included in the architecture. No memory management support is provided.

A communications element is integral to the processor, and is implemented with 8 dma channels. The communication element handles interprocessor data messages. In the message format, 20 bits contain a destination address, 4 bits are assigned for message control. A 32 bit word format is used.

The external memory interface is of a Von Neumann style, with a 64 bit wide data path, and 24 bit address. Since iWarps are designed to be used in large parallel networks, the small address space only effects local memory, not total system memory. A 40 MHz clock is used.

General purpose instructions on the iWarp are 32 bits in size. Following the VLIW philosophy, the iWarp also uses a 96 bit compute and access instruction format, with a 32 bit general purpose format. A single VLIW instruction can perform a floating add, floating multiple, two memory address computations, and a memory access. Loop decrement and branch evaluation takes two cycles.

Integer math instructions perform add and subtract. Floating point operations include add, subtract, multiply, divide, log, square root, comparison, and conversion. Shift/bit manipulation instructions include AND, OR,

XOR, XNOR, find high bit, and set and reset bit. Flow control is implemented by calls, branches, and supervisor calls.

The register file contains 128 32-bit locations, It is 15-way ported, and can support 9 reads and 6 writes in one clock time. This feature allows both the computation agent and communication elements to access the registers simultaneously. The local memory unit has a 24 bit address bus and a 64 bit data bus. The program store unit implements a 1 kilobyte instruction cache, and has start-up and system routines in ROM. The integer and floating point units operate in parallel. The floating adder is not pipelined, and operates in parallel with the multiplier. Single precision requires 2 cycles, and double precision requires 4 cycles from either unit.

Supported data types on the iWarp include bytes, half words, words (32 b), and double words. iWarp tools are hosted on the Sun platform, and include a c and a Fortran optimizing compiler, with language extensions for parallelism. Support tools also include a linker, debug monitor, and run time environment. Math and Unix system call libraries are available.

Full IEEE single and double precision floating point is provided in the iWarp. The floating point unit uses the general register file on the iWarp chip. The on-chip cache includes 1 kilobyte. I/O is memory mapped.

Intel's i80860

This section will discuss Intel's i860 chip - called a Cray on a chip. The i860 addresses the high end graphics and computation enhancement markets. Box level products based on the i860 address simulation and modeling, animation, virtual reality, image processing, and other high end, computationally intensive applications.

There are two members of the i860 family, the XR and the XP. The i860 processor, modestly described by Intel as "a Cray on a Chip", achieves high levels of integer, floating point, and 3 d graphics performance simultaneously. The i860XR is a pure 64 bit risc design at the 1 million transistor level, using 1 micron, double metal processes in CHMOS. The i860XR achieves the same scalar performance and one fourth to one half of the vector performance of the first Cray machine, which is, of course, now in the Smithsonian. The era of the desktop supercomputer is truly here. By using a superscalar architecture, up to 3 instructions/clock can be executed. The on-chip 8k data and 4k instruction caches have very high bandwidth due to wide internal data paths. The caches are two-way set-associative, and utilize a write-back scheme. The instruction caches's data path is 64 bits, while the data cache's is 128 bits. The chip's external data bus is 64 bits in width, but secondary cache is not supported. The chip is of a Harvard architecture internally, but has a unified memory architecture externally. Dual instruction mode, in which a 64 bit wide integer and floating point pair is fetched and executed, is a variation of the long instruction word format. The chip utilizes a load/store architecture, with on-chip transfers taking advantage of the wide internal data paths.

Intel's second generation 860, the XP variant, extends the performance envelope a considerable distance using 0.8 micron, triple level CHMOS to achieve a density of 2.5 million transistors. The new chip is binary compatible with the previous, but doubles the performance figures by adding support for second level cache, faster busses, larger on-chip caches, as well as upping the clock speed. Multiprocessing support is added in the form of hardware support for bus snooping for cache consistency, and bus arbitration features.

The integer unit achieves the one instruction per clock goal. Integer register bypassing is available, where the result of an operation is available as an input to the next stage in the pipeline without a register write/read. A single-cycle loop instruction is included. The integer unit can handle loads, stores, and loop control, while the floating point unit multiplies and adds.

The floating point unit uses dedicated 3 stage pipelines for the add and multiply units. The unit supports the data types, operations, and exceptions defined in the IEEE 754 standard format.

The built-in 3D graphics unit also uses pipelined techniques to speed up operations, such as management of Z-buffers, and color shading. These techniques are used in shading and hidden line removal algorithms for high performance graphics. Display techniques such as pixel interpolation and Gouraud shading are supported by hardware graphics primitives, high speed floating point multiply, and vectorization of operations. In addition, the graphics unit can add and subtract 64 bit integers.

DMA handshake protocols also provide for multiprocessor bus master-ship hand off. A single interrupt pin is provided, and the external interrupt can be masked in software. The i860 MMU design is borrowed from the 386 family. The XR includes hardware support for cache consistency, bus snooping, and arbitration.

The 860 bus architecture is Harvard internally, unified externally. Bus width is 64 bits. On chip write buffers are used.

Upon reset, execution begins at the high memory address. The program must initialize control registers, and the caches must be flushed, although they are marked as invalidated. Execution begins at the supervisor level.

A 1 times clock is used, 25 - 40 MHz for the XR, 40 - 50 MHZ for the XP.

Hardware support for testing is provided in the i860 parts, with a compliance with the IEEE P1149.1/D6 specification, and a test access port (tap).

Second level (external) cache for the XP part is supplied

by the companion 82495XP cache controller in conjunction with the 82490XP cache RAM. The secondary cache is unified. Cache write-through is supported.

In the i860 instruction set, all instructions are 32 bits in size, and either a register or a control format. The integer math instructions include add and subtract on up to 32 bit entities. 64 bit integers are handled in the graphics unit. Floating point instructions include add, subtract, multiply, reciprocal, square root, compares and conversions. Pipelined floating operations, possible because the adder and multiplier are separate, include add/multiply, subtract/multiply, multiply/add, and multiply/subtract. Load/store operations operate on integer, floating, or pixel items. Left and right shifts are provided, and the AND, OR, and XOR logical operations.

Flow control instructions include call subroutine, branch conditional and unconditional, and a software trap instruction. Special graphics instructions support Z-buffer and pixel operations. The XP provides additional operations for load and store I/O, and cache flush.

On the i860 chips are found 32 32-bit integer registers and 32 32-bit floating point registers. R0 is read as zero, as are F0 and F1. There are twelve control registers, including the processor status register (PSR), the floating point status register (FSR), the extended PSR (EPSR), the data breakpoint register (DB), the directory base register, the fault instruction register, the bus error address register, the concurrency control register, and 4 privilege registers P0-P4.

The PSR contains current state information, including condition codes, the loop condition code, a shift count, a pixel size indicator, bits for data access trapping, indicators of interrupt mode and previous interrupt mode, and user/supervisor mode and previous user/supervisor mode. In addition, 5 trap flags are included. The other fields are Delayed Switch, dual instruction mode, and kill next floating point instruction.

The EPSR contains more information about the state, including the processor type and stepping number (manufacturing variation), endian setting, on-chip data cache size, bus error flag, overflow flag, trap indicators for delayed instruction, auto increment, and pipeline usage, a write-protect bit for the directory and page table entries, and interlock bit for trap sequences.

The floating point status register contains information about the current state of the floating point processor, including rounding modes, trap status, overflow and underflow from the adder or multiplier, and trap enables. The data breakpoint register stores the breakpoint address if a trap is taken. The Directory base register is used to control caching, address translation and bus options. It contains the 20 high order bits of the page directory, the fields for the cache replacement/flushing control, a bus lock bit, a virtual address enable, a DRAM page size indicator, and a code size bit, to allow bootstrapping from 8 bit wide devices. The fault instruction register is used to hold the address of the instruction causing a trap. Similarly, the bus error address register holds the address for the bus cycle during which a bus error or parity error was detected. The concurrency control register is used to enable or disable the concurrency control feature for multiprocessing, and to specify the controlled address space.

Byte ordering is select-able in software, with the normal mode being little-endian. The controlling bit is contained in the extended PSP register.

In the i860, most data types are compatible with those of the 80x86 family. Data types include 8 to 64 bit integers, and 32, 64 or 128 bit floating point operands. The i860XP pixel processor operates on 8, 16, or 32 bit data items. In a 16 bit wide pixel, there are 6 bits of intensity for red and green, and 5 bits for blue. The 32 bit format has 8 bits for each color, plus 8 bits for general use.

Unix and OSF/1 are available on the i860 platform, with a full suite of compilers and software tools. The early i860's met with little acceptance in the market place until adequate software toolsets were provided for code development. The software tools and development environments are now mature for the i860. Toolsets include the "c" language, Fortran-77, a vectorizer, associated graphics and math libraries, ADA, the assembler, linker, loader, and librarian, and are available from Intel and various 3rd. party vendors. MASS860 is the vendor organization.

Floating point is the i860 architecture's strong point, with double precision adds taking 3 cycles, and double precision multiplies, four. A pipelined mode for vectorized operations allows one result per cycle (after latency). The adder and multiplier can operate simultaneously. Hardware support for square root and reciprocal are provided. The floating point unit has its own set of 32 registers. IEEE format is supported. All four rounding modes of the IEEE standard are supported. There is no divide operation per se, but a reciprocal and a square root are calculated by Newton-Raphson techniques. In dual mode, an add/subtract and a multiply can be done in parallel.

The 860XR cache is 2-way set associative, and includes 4 kbytes for instruction, and 8 kbytes for data. Caches are virtually mapped.

The 860XP uses 4-way set associative 16k byte internal instruction and data caches. Both virtual and physical tags are kept. The MESI protocol is supported for multiprocessor cache consistency. The 860XP MMU has been extended to add a 4 Megabyte page size. Compatibility with paged 32 bit addressing on the 386/486 model is maintained. The external datapath remains 64 bits in width with posted writes, a three stage read pipelines, and a one clock burst bus. New control registers are added to support multiprocessing and other operating system functions. Write back and write through policies are selectable for the on-chip I- and D- caches. The MESI protocol for cache coherency is supported by the XP.

The on-chip MMU is based on the i80386 design, and provides two level paging, and 4k page size. User and Supervisor mode protection is provided. The mmu uses a 64 entry TLB that is 4 way set associative. Hardware support is provided for TLB miss exceptions. On the XP, there is an additional 4 megabyte page size, dynamically selectable. Address translation can be enabled or disabled, and I/O occupies a separate space. The page table includes bits for present, writable, user/supervisor, write-thru, cacheable, accessed, and dirty.

In the i860, there are 8 types of exceptions. These include instruction fault, floating point fault (following the IEEE model), instruction or data access fault, parity or bus error, reset, or external interrupt. Interrupt vectors are used.

Alpha

The DEC Alpha chips is a 64-bit, superscalar, superpipelined architecture. It uses the Load/Store approach, and supports 32 integer and 32 floating point registers. R31 and F31 are defined as zero. The architecture is a derivative of the circa 1986 PRISM. The project started in 1988, with first silicon by 1992. It has found use in DEC's own workstations, and the Cray MPP.

Addressing is 64-bit virtual, 34 bit physical, and is little-endian. The chip uses register scoreboarding and result bypassing for speed. There are no condition codes. 128 bit internal data paths are used. Other optimization techniques included in the design include read/write re-ordering, branch prediction, and out-of-order execution.

The instructions are all 32 bits long, with a 6-bit opcode. There are four classes of instruction: PALcode, conditional branch, load/store, and operate/floating. The PALcode is an instruction set extension via hardware abstraction layer. It resides in ROM, and supports VAX family instructions. Multiprocessor coherency is provided by cache snooping.

Before the full power of the Alpha chips could be unleashed, DEC was bought out by Compaq Computer. Production of the Alpha was shifted to Samsung. The Alpha Design Group became Alpha Processor, INC which later became API Networks, Inc. Later, Compaq dumped the Alpha design.

There were several models of the Alpha chip. The 21064 featured a 7-stage integer pipeline, and a 10-stage pipeline for floating point. It had 4 functional units, the integer, floating, branch, and load/store. It also had an integral MMU. The 21066 added integrated dram support. The 21164 was the last model. It operated at 366 through 800 Mhz, and was fabricated by Samsung. An "A" version added video-related instructions, and a "B" version extended the clock to 1 Ghz. The 21264 was to have out-of-order execution for up to 80 instructions, but by this time, the Design team was disbanding. The 21364, on the drawing board, was targeted to scalable multiprocessor systems, and had onboard switching/routing for I/O.

MIPS

Meaning "Microprocessor without interlocking stages," the MIPS architecture was the brainchild of John Hennessy at Stanford. It was produced by multiple manufacturers, and addressed the workstation market. MIPS, the company, was eventually bought by SGI. MIPS was the keeper of the architectural specification of the chips, with various company's producing variants.

There were several architectural models of the MIPS chip. The R-2000 was a 32-bit load/store machine with associated MMU and floating point chips. The R-3000 was also 32-bit, but was produced in various versions for the embedded market. The R-4000 was a 64-bit machine with integral coprocessors.

The R-2000

The R-2000 chip was an integer cpu with a 5-stage pipeline, and 32 32-bit registers. Register zero was defined as zero, and Register 31 contained a return address. All instructions were a standard 32-bits in length for ease of decode and pipelining. The architecture allowed for 1 to 4 coprocessors, tightly coupled. CR0 was defined as the system control processor, the mmu.

CR1 was the floating point processor. The five-stage pipeline included stations for fetch, decode, ALU, memory access, and write.

The R-3000

The R-3000 processor was a Harvard architecture internally, having separate data and instruction paths. It supported multiprocessing. There was an associated R-3010 floating point coprocessor. Many embedded variations of the R-3000 architecture were produced.

The R-4000

The R-4000 was a true 64-bit chip, with 64-bit address bus, registers, ALU, and data paths. It was a dual-issue, 8-stage pipeline design.

The MIPS architecture supported both little-endian or big-endian mode, selectable at reset.

PowerPC

The Power-PC architecture resulted in a collaboration between Motorola and IBM. Motorola contributed the 88000 RISC architecture, and IBM threw in parts of the ROMPS, RiscPC, and Power architecture. The result was an architecture to challenge the Intel IA-32 and IA-64.

The IBM POWER (performance optimization with enhanced RISC) architecture was circa 1990, and was designed to run the Unix variant AIX. The two processors that resulted were the RIOS I and RIOS II, before the Design was blended into the PowerPC. Motorola's 88k was a risc architecture as a follow-on to their 68k cisc processor. There was a 88100 cpu chip and an associated 88200 cache control chip. The cpu hosted 5 execution units and 4 pipelines. It was a Harvard architecture. There were 51 instructions, later expanded to 66, and 32 32-bit registers. The 88k found use in BBN's Butterfly parallel processor, with 504 cpu's.

The Power-pc was 3-way super-scalar, with separate integer, floating point, and branch processing. It supported out-of-order execution and hardware branch prediction. The memory management unit converted 52-bit virtual addresses to 32-bit physical addresses. The internal cache was a unified structure in the early units, moving to a separate or Harvard cache structure later. Multiple processors were supported. The PowerPC could dynamically order the load/store traffic at run time.

From a programmer's point of view, the PowerPC was a load/store architecture. All addressing was register indirect. There was an interruptible string move instruction. There were 32 general purpose integer registers, and 32 floating point registers. Byte ordering was selectable, with big-endian being the default. There were 184 instructions, and both a user and supervisor mode.

The PowerPC 601 was the first generation part, running from 50-120 Mhz. It had a unified cache of 32 kbytes. The part was used by both Apple computer and IBM. The PowerPC 602 project was to be able to execute both PPC and Intel IA-21 instruction sets. It was never completed.

The PowerPC reached 66-300 Mhz clock speeds, and introduced the Harvard cache architecture. The PowerPC 604 ran from 100 to 350 Mhz, and the cache size was 64k.

The PowerPC G3, models 740 and 750, featured dual caches of 32k each. The G4 introduced the AltiVec instructions. These were for multimedia data, similar to Intel's MMX extension. The AltiVec instructions, 160 in number, had their own separate 32 registers, each 128 bits wide. The G4 ran at 350 to 1100 Mhz, and went to a 7-stage pipeline.

IBM variants of the architecture included the Power3 which was a 64-bit machine and became the basis for the RS6000 servers, and the Power$, which stretched the operating frequency to 1Ghz. Motorola produced embedded versions of the PPC architecture for the automotive and communications industry's. A typical MPC 5xx series embedded part included support of the PPC instruction set, integrated ram, flash, a timer, serial I/O and A/D functions.

IA-32

The Instruction Set Architecture, 32 bits, (IA-32) formed the basis for Intel's chips from the 80386 to the Pentium IV and beyond. The earlier Intel processors were 8 or 16 bits. This architecture was extended to 32 bits in the 80386 and would be extended to 64 bits later.

IA-32 features variable length instructions (which are a

challenge to pipeline), a small number of registers, multiple, complicated instruction modes. It is then a CISC, not a RISC architecture. In later models, it would be recognized the instruction set had reached its limits of optimization, and dynamic instruction translation to an internal risc instruction set for execution would be used. The CISC instruction set did provide support for legacy code, which was an important issue for Intel.

From the initial 80386 32-bit architecture, the '486 incorporated the floating point unit internally, and the Pentium expanded the implementation to dual-issue superscalar. There were two integer units and one floating point. Of course, the amount of cache grew as time went on, from 8k in the '486 to 16k in the Pentium I, to 32 k in the Pentium II.

Pipelining is a nightmare to implement with variable length instructions. From the '486 to the P6, a 5 stage pipeline was used. The Pentium IV issues 6 instructions per clock cycle into a 20 stage pipeline. However, these are NOT 80x86 instructions. They are risc instructions, that the 80x86 instructions have been dynamically translated into.

Other company's implemented the IA-32 into their chips. AMD, for example, took the basic architecture and added techniques for optimization from their 29k risc chip to produce the K5 chip. The follow-on K6 has a RISC86 core, with instruction translation. Next, the Athlon incorporated 3 integer, 3 floating, and 3 address calculation pipelines. The integer pipes are 10-stage, and the floating is 15-stage.

Cyrix used the IA-32 with register renaming and speculative execution. NexGen features the dynamic translation of the 80x86 instructions into internal 104-bit RISC instructions. WinChip featured branch prediction.

The PowerPC-615 could execute PowerPC or IA-32 instructions, by translation, The Toshiba Tigershark could translated IA-32 instructions to SPARC format, dynamically.

The 64-bit machines use advanced optimization techniques. An HP/Intel design uses VLIW (Very Long Instruction Words) to contain 3 instructions in 128 bits. Techniques in instruction-level parallelism include superscalar implementations and instruction re-ordering in hardware.

MPMS Approaches & techniques

This section discusses various approaches and techniques used in MPMS design. First, we'll examine where the bottlenecks are in processing, to derive a set of targets to optimize. The next bottleneck to be encountered is in I/O, and there are various approaches to be explored. We'll look at rate balancing, then some concepts of MPMS. We next need to examine how these MPMS characteristics are achieved.

Where is the bottleneck?

In any scheme designed to improve performance, we need to ensure that we are concentrating on those system elements that need optimization. First, we must derive requirements by examining where the bottlenecks are in our problem set. Do we need faster integer or floating point calculations? Do we need faster double precision, or graphics manipulation? Or, are we bound in the amount of information we can access, not in the amount we can process? Scientific problems tend to emphasize floating point, whereas business data processing tends to emphasize I/O intensive database operations.

The 1.1 Problem

As an introduction to the need for communication among processors, consider a problem that takes 1.1 times the capability of the processor you have available. This is referred to as the 1.1 problem. Since the problem is, by definition, bigger than 1 processor can handle, you need two processors. but, getting two processors to cooperate on one problem is a major headache. To begin with, how do they communicate? Shared memory is one solution, but this takes away from the available memory bandwidth for instruction fetch, and doesn't work well beyond 4 processors. Then, how do we solve the communication problem for the 4.1 problem? More importantly, how do we achieve an architectural solution that is scalable from 1.1 to x.1? And, scalable means scalable in processing and communication power. Contention for communication resources such as shared buses adds the complexity and overhead of arbitration.

SMP, Clusters, and Parallel processing

What does "Symmetric" Multiprocessing mean?

1. MPPs scale to (an arbitrary threshold of) 32 cpu's. An MPP is defined by the Gartner Group as having more than 100 cpu's. SMP's are defined as shared memory multiprocessors having identical hardware, and executing identical software. So, are all SMP's of a shared memory architecture? THE IBM SP series are not, and neither is the Cray SS. These are borderline SMP's.

2. MPPs allow a single instantiation of multiprocessing programs – for instance MPPs run one copy of the operating system with micro-kernels on all other processor; and similarly for Oracle, for instance. This is more unusual for SMP's, but this is not a differentiator. It does make SMP's less 'S'.

3. MPPs have hardware and software mechanisms for high-speed, efficient interprocessor communication, which allows scalability beyond the arbitrary threshold of 1.

4. SMP's are grown upward from workstation manufacturers; MPP's are made by wanna-be supercomputer manufacturers. SMP's start at 1

cpu, go to 2, 4, 8...Where MPP machines are designed from the start to be (massive) 1024 or 4096 cpu resources units...Storage and memory resources are designed to be commensurate.

Concurrency and parallelism are features of the real world, and thus of simulations and models of the world, at galactic or sub-nuclear dimensions. Events occur simultaneously, and in 3 spatial and 1 time dimension. Nothing happens in ordered, sequential mode, except in digital simulations. When truly parallel events are modeled by sequential means, artificial constraints must be added to allow the "real-time" interaction of events.

Parallelism can be achieved by providing enough hardware to simultaneously calculate all parts of the problem in 1 time step, or by using 1 computation engine that switches fast enough to look like it is calculating simultaneously. The problem must lend itself to being decomposed into composite parts. The problem must be commensurate with a parallel solution approach. Not all problems are, and of those that are, each required a unique set of computation/communication resources and topologies for optimum performance. There are no optimum general purpose parallel processor architectures. For specific problem domains, an optimum processor topology can be devised.

Parallel processing can be considered as shared resource or distributed resource. Shared resource systems use a common bus, memory, or other element among homogeneous processors. Concurrency is achieved by time sharing. A distributed system partitions and allocates the problem across resources. The main problems to be overcome are: how to partition the problem, and how to allocate it.

Processor - I/O balance

Most problem domains have an inherent requirement for processor throughput and communication bandwidth. In embedded applications, we shall see that the metric of interest is usually interrupt response determinism and latency. In large scientific or engineering problems, it is usually MIPS or Megaflops. But, we also have to consider memory capacity and speed. No matter how many registers we have on-chip, we are unlikely to have enough to be able to invert a 100k x 100k matrix without an access to memory. What we want is enough registers to minimize cache accesses, enough cache to minimize main memory accesses, and enough main memory to minimize disk accesses. For high external I/O bandwidth processing, such as video data, we need an architecture that lets the data flow through the processor, because we won't have enough memory for more than a few seconds worth of data. However, we can examine the inherent "graininess" of the problem to decide whether the problem can be partitioned and operated upon in parallel,

Let's look at some definitions. If we have more than one processor working on a problem, we have multiprocessing.

Although faster uni-processors are one answer, and certainly the trend of technology, they do not provide an answer to the essential problem of getting around the von Neumann Bottleneck. This is, in essence, a communications channel restriction problem between the processor and memory. Coupled with Flynn's anomaly, that states that one processor element can only do one thing at a time, an upper bound is placed on the throughput of uni-processor systems.

Multiprocessor systems tend to convert compute-bound problems into I/O bound problems, by stressing the interprocessor interconnect topology. A usual solution is the use of high bandwidth channels such as shared memory. A key interprocessor communication question to answer is whether the communication resource is shared in time (TDM) or in space (cross-bar switching). However, regardless of the scheme used, the interprocessor communication channel has an upper limit (ala Shannon), and most processors are not well balanced in terms of processing capability with respect to I/O capability. A metric in this area is the number of operations that can be performed on each byte of incoming data, in mega-ops per second per megabyte per second, simplified to operations/byte.

An example of a tightly coupled multiprocessor system that addresses the processor-I/O design trade-offs very well is the Transputer architecture from Inmos Corp. It is inherently modular. We will discuss an overview of the architecture later, but a key point is that one or more

Transputers can be configured to implement any of the various types of system architecture we might like to address :

taxonomy of processors addressed by Transputers:

> SISD - 1 Transputer
> SIMD - multiple Transputers, running same
> program
> MIMD - multiple Transputers, multiple data
> streams
> MISD - multiple Transputers, different programs, 1
> data   stream

In addition, the T-800 achieves a metric of over 3 ops/byte, showing that even in maximum I/O flow, a minimum of 3 computer operations can be performed on each data byte. Contrast this with the TMS 320C040 Parallel Processing DSP (Digital Signal Processor) from Texas Instruments, which achieves a metric of 2.

One approach to solving increasing complex problems with increasingly capable hardware is simply to wait. Given enough time, sufficiently complex hardware for the problem domain will emerge. However, it is increasingly apparent that software development lags hardware to the extent that software tools do not emerge until the hardware is obsolete by at least two generations. Also, the capabilities of any given hardware design can be exceeded by computational problems of interest well into the foreseeable future. At any given point of technological complexity, a cluster of coordinated processors can outperform a single processor. Thus, faced with a seemingly inexhaustible complex problem domain, along with industry emphasis on hardware development, we need to tackle both the software and the communication domains to better utilize the hardware available at any given point.

Computation rate should balance I/O rate

The Transputer offers a solution to the rate balancing problem in multiprocessor designs. Consider a computational problem, for example, image texture analysis, which requires more resources than a single processor can provide. In adding a second or subsequent processors, we achieve diminishing returns in processing power, because we have created communication requirements between processors with band limited channels. Ahmdahl's Law says we get less than 1 unit of incremental processor power per added processor. In most real designs, the curve of incremental processor power per added processor displays a sharp fall-off. However, a Transputer is designed with a good balance of processing power (10 mips, 1 mflop) and communication ability 4 x 20 Mbps in and out simultaneously. Thus, each added processor can add nearly a complete increment of processing power to the system. In one benchmark of an essentially compute-bound problem we implemented, 17 processors add almost 17 times the power of one processor. Of course, the problem in question must be commensurate with a parallel solution, but a surprising number of real world problems are. Essentially, we feel that the communications topology of the parallel processor is specified by the problem characteristics. This proposed effort is to quantify that specification.

Recent work by Texas Instruments in their TMS 320 line has attempted to produce -interfaced parallel ports. However, this still does not achieve the processor:I/O balance designed into the Transputer. The TMS line is presented as digital signal processors, not general purpose processors, which limit their application in many cases of interest to science and engineering.
MPMS concepts

The basic concepts of the MPMS paradigm are presented below.

Performance limitations of conventional architectures

This section discusses the limitations of conventional architectures that are addressed by MPMS machines.

The Tera-flop goal and the Peta-flop Possibility

The Holy Grail of scientific massively parallel machines is presently a tera-flop, or 10^{12} floating point operations per second. This will scope many of the "Grand Challenge" problems postulated in the 1990's. Machines that achieve a tera-flop began to appear in 1994, although a sustainable tera-flop will be more time in coming

A 1994 workshop examined the required basis technology for Peta-operations (10^15).

Architectural Approaches for performance

This section examines the system level architectural approaches used for performance in MPMS machines.

The Evolution of MPMS

Machines built up from multiple microprocessors have been around since there were more than one microprocessor to work with. Machines built up from 256 Z-80's had popularity because of the low cost of the building blocks. But, putting massive numbers of low cost processors together in one box is not the hard part - getting them all to work on the same problem is. CISC processors lend themselves better to a distributed memory scheme.

NEC announced in early 1993 a parallel machine built up from multiple MIPS R4400 processors.

Development and Debug

Tools for Parallel Architectures

We must consider the software tools to develop parallel applications to be of equal or greater importance with the hardware. Users require compiler support for both C and

Fortran. We would like to have canned libraries of vector & matrix operations. We also could use vectorizing preprocessing compilers. First, we have to visit the topic of open source versus proprietary.

Open Source versus Proprietary

This is a topic we need to discuss before we get very far into software. It is not a technical topic, but concerns your right to use (and/or own, modify) software. It's those software licenses you click to agree with, and never read. That's what the intellectual property lawyers are betting on.

Software and software tools are available in proprietary and open source versions. Open source software is free and widely available, and may be incorporated into your system. It is available under license, which generally says that you can use it, but derivative products must be made available under the same license. This presents a problem if it is mixed with purchased, licensed commercial software, or a level of exclusivity is required. Major government agencies such as the Department of Defense and NASA have policies related to the use of Open Source software.

Adapting a commercial or open source operating system to a particular problem domain can be tricky. Usually, the commercial operating systems need to be used "as-is" and the source code is not available. The software can usually be configured between well-defined limits, but there will be no visibility of the internal workings. For the open source situation, there will be a multitude of source code modules and libraries that can be configured and customized, but the process is complex. The user can also write new modules in this case.

Large corporations or government agencies sometimes have problems incorporating open source products into their projects. Open Source did not fit the model of how they have done business traditionally. They are issues and lingering doubts. Many Federal agencies have developed Open Source policies. NASA has created an open source license, the NASA Open Source Agreement (NOSA), to address these issues. It has released software under this license, but the Free Software Foundation had some issues with the terms of the license. The Open Source Initiative (www.opensource.org) maintains the definition of Open Source, and certifies licenses such as the NOSA.

The GNU General Public License (GPL) is the most widely used free software license. It guarantees end users the freedoms to use, study, share, copy, and modify the software. Software that ensures that these rights are retained is called free software. The license was originally written by Richard Stallman of the Free Software Foundation (FSF) for the GNU project in 1989. The GPL is a *copyleft* license, which means that derived works can only be distributed under the same license terms. This is in distinction to permissive free software licenses, of which the BSD licenses are the standard examples. Copyleft is in counterpoint to traditional copyright. Proprietary software "poisons" free software, and cannot be included or integrated with it, without abandoned the GPL. The GPL covers the GNU/linux operating systems and most of the GNU/linux-based applications.

A Vendor's software tools and operating system or application code is usually proprietary intellectual property. It is unusual to get the source code to examine, at least without binding legal documents and additional funds. Along with this, you do get the vendor support. An alternative is open source code, which is in the public domain. There are a series of licenses covering open source code usage, including the Creative Commons License, the gnu public license, copyleft, and others. Open Source describes a collaborative environment for development and testing. Use of open source code carries with it an implied responsibility to "pay back" to the community. Open Source is not necessarily free.

The Open source philosophy is sometimes at odds with the rigidized procedures evolved to ensure software performance and reliability. Offsetting this is the increased visibility into the internals of the software packages, and control over the entire software package. Besides application code, operating systems such as GNU/linux and bsd can be open source. The programming language Python is open source. The popular web server Apache is also open source.

Vectorizing Compilers

The vectorizer pre-processes source code to convert standard statements and calls into vector processing calls from a supplied library. These library functions make maximal use of the specific pipeline and parallel architecture of the chip. Generally, a data dependency analysis is performed on loops to identify sections to be converted to library calls. The library must then be linked to the compiled code. The vectorizer must sometimes remove scalar optimization, which can mask vectorization.

Taking advantage of the vector libraries optimizes performance and throughput, and allows achievement of the full pipeline efficiency and multiple execution per clock potential of the hardware.

Parallelizing Compilers

The vectorizer pre-processes source code to convert standard statements and calls into vector processing calls from a supplied library. These library functions make maximal use of the pipeline and parallel architecture of the chip. Generally, a data dependency analysis is performed on loops to identify sections to be converted to library calls. The library must then be linked to the compiled code. The vectorizer must sometimes remove scalar optimization, which can mask vectorization.

Taking advantage of the vector libraries optimizes performance and throughput, and allows achievement of the full pipeline efficiency and multiple execution per clock potential of the hardware. Such ancillary software tools as profilers and debugging tools are also desirable.

Several software tools for Intel's i860 architecture have emerged. One is the Zephyr distributed programming tool from Paralogic (Bethlehem, Pa.). The product runs on a SUN 4. Paralogic also has the BERT product, which is a parallel Fortran compiler for Fortran-77. A similar product for C/C++ called ERNIE was supposed to be available in the 3rd quarter, 1993. BERT, derived from previous Russian work , currently only produces code for the Transputer. Version 2 will address different hosts and targets.

Microway has a wide range of software tools available, both their own products, and third party. Of interest are the Numerical Algorithms, and the VAST-2 vectorizer. Transtech has the i860 toolset for their board, based on similar architectural models from the Transputer world.
PVM

The Parallel Virtual Machine (PVM) software package, developed at the Oak Ridge National Laboratory of the Department of Energy, links heterogeneous computers together into one computational resource. It operates on equipment from Sun, Cray, Alliant, IBM, TMC, Intel, and others. The PVM software is in the public domain, and available on the Internet for downloading. Customized commercial versions of PVM are available from various vendors such as Craysoft, IBM, and Convex, which are optimized for their environments.

PVM is transparent to the type of individual machine (shared vs. distributed memory, vector, risc, etc.), and to the interconnect method. PVM software is on each node of the configuration, and presents a virtual, unified computational resource to the user. Library routines for programs in C or Fortran are part of PVM. These routines, when linked with the user code, provide PVM connectivity to the user. Routines are provided for communication and process synchronization.

PVM allows the collection of a number of existing computational resources into one large resource as needed. For example, a heavy use computational job can take advantage of slack or idle time on machines on a network. Alternately, collections of workstations can be linked at night or over the weekend into one large machine to address batch jobs. A graphical interface tool for visualization within the PVM environment is available as HeNCE (Heterogeneous Network Computing Environment).

Development Environments

This section discusses development environments for parallel software, such as the TDS from Inmos, and systems such as the Parasoft Express, and Linda.

Benchmarking

Benchmarks are so misused to compare computer systems that a few cautions are in order. Benchmarks represent an artificial environment that does not model any particular application. They are rough estimates; not absolute measures of performance. The best benchmarks are actual programs from out of your environment. But, industry standard benchmarks can indicate what processors deserve a second look. The indicated candidates should then be benchmarked with your own code.

Integer benchmarks include the Dhrystone, developed in ADA by R. Weicker 1984, and Stanford integer suite: samples of code from various applications, developed by Stanford's Computer Science Department.

Floating point benchmarks include the Whetstone, developed in the late 1960's by Curnow and Wichman at National Physical Lab, Whetstone, England. It includes transcendentals, arrays computations, etc. and is not vectorizable. The Linpack was developed by Jack Dongarra at Argonne National Labs in 1978, and is floating point intensive. It is intended to give users of Linpack software (basic linear algebra package) an idea of run times.

The SPEC (Systems Performance Evaluation Cooperative) benchmarks come in both flavors, and are widely cited The SPEC-fp floating point benchmark is single precision.

Interconnect

This section will discuss the architectural approaches in

using large numbers of microprocessors connected together into one machine. Although most entrants in this arena choose to take advantage of the economies of scale of merchant RISC chips, some choose to design their own. Notable among the latter are KSR and nCube. The rationale for the custom design is that the additional "glue" logic required around the off-the-shelf chip to allow it to be integrated into a system provides a level of complication at the system level. Single chip MPMS nodes such as nCube's allow for extremely simple, and thus inexpensive nodes. The correct approach is not obvious, and, as in many cases, it may turn out that there are several correct answers. The success or failure of competing approaches depend on a myriad of factors, some technical, some financial, some marketing. We will address all of the approaches in subsequent sections.

Topology of Interconnection of Elements

In this section, we address architectural approaches to coordinating the use of multiple processors. Most of these approaches will work with any underlying technology, and are useful after the maximum speed of a single processor in a given technology has been wrung out.

One approach to solving increasing complex problems with increasingly capable hardware is simply to wait. Given enough time, sufficiently complex hardware for the problem domain will emerge. However, it is increasingly apparent that software development lags hardware to the extent that software tools do not emerge until the hardware is obsolete by at least two generations. Also, the capabilities of any given hardware design will be exceeded by computational problems of interest well into the foreseeable future. At any given point of technological complexity, a cluster of coordinated processors can outperform a single processor. Thus, faced with a seemingly inexhaustible complex problem domain, along with industry emphasis on hardware development, we need to tackle both the software and the communication domains to better utilize the hardware available at any given point. Software will be discussed in section 4. Here, we want to discuss the critical issue of communications among elements.

The bottleneck to getting more than one processor to work on a given problem domain at one time is the communications. There is an upper bound in a bus-oriented, shared memory SMP systems, arising from the communication limit of the bus interconnect (a classic Shannon channel limit). Clusters of computers also suffer from an interprocessor communication limit, from the LAN-like interconnect. Some MPP's are like clusters in a box.

Shared memory MPP's usually do not have a homogeneous communication environment, due to communication bandwidth restrictions. A two tier communications architecture is used, with shared memory intrabox, and a lan type point-point link for interbox messaging. Since MPP machines have to scale to thousands of processors, a distributed memory scheme is usually chosen. Another approach is to cluster SMP's. Data sharing is the key, and the critical issue for large parallel relational database applications. The performance will be made (or broken) by the sophistication of the interconnection scheme. Speed and latency are of critical importance. Latency predominates for short messages

In the interconnect hierarchy, the node-node connection is frequently made via shared memory. Thus, a node may be an SMP architecture in its own right, with two or four processor elements. this approach does not scale well beyond about 16 processors. The node-node communication is tightly coupled.

Between nodes, a loosely coupled message passing scheme is usually employed. This uses a LAN-like architecture, which can take one of many topological forms. Popular are the mesh, torus, hypercube, and tree. The following table shows the approaches taken by some of the major vendors. Each of these interconnect approaches will be examined in the subsequent sections.

Interconnect Topology of some MIMD machines

Company	Machine	interconnect
Convex	Exemplar	torus
Cray	T3D	torus
KSR	KSR-2	torus
Intel SSD	Paragon	mesh
Meiko	CS-2	fat tree

nCube	nCube-3	hypercube
Tandem	K10K	torus
TMC	CM-5	fat tree

The Mesh

The mesh is an n-dimensional grid, with processors at the vertices of the grid. If we assume that communications delay is linear in distance, then the mesh topology is very efficient. 'Distance' is the metric that expresses the communication cost between nodes.

The mesh architecture is favored by Intel for their Paragon series, based on work done at CalTech. The chip instantiation is the iMRC (mesh router component). This allows vendors to interconnect chips such as the i860 and Pentium.

The early iPSC series uses as many as one-hundred twenty-eight 40-mhz i860xr chips. Special I/O nodes used a shared I/O design are based on the i80386. The internal networked, called 'Direct-Connect', provided bi-directional 5.6 Mbyte/second channels in a switched configuration. The Paragon machine scales to 1024 of the i860XP processors, arranged in SMP type, 4 processor nodes. Each node can have up to 128 Mbytes of memory. The inter-processor communication architecture scales as nodes are added. A 2D mesh configuration, with a mesh router for each node, provides a message passing architecture with a bi-directional node-node bandwidth of 200 Mbytes per second, and a latency of 40 Nanoseconds per node hop.

Intel's Paragon machine scales to 1024 of the 50 Mhz. i860XP processors, arranged in SMP-type, 4 processor nodes. Each node can have up to 128 mbytes of memory. The nodes are interconnected in a mesh. Future Paragon models will incorporate the Pentium chip or subsequent, and development on the 64 bit successor to the i860 will be (or has been) dropped. The "Touchstone Delta" System is a one of a kind system built for the California Institute of Technology using 520 of the i860 chips.

The Hypercube

The hypercube is an efficient topology for interconnection, because it provides a large number of interconnects, while keeping the maximum distance between any two nodes small. The number of nodes is restricted to a power of two, although incomplete hypercubes are possible. Each apex of the n-dimensional cube is a node. This allows a direct connection to each nearest neighbor in n-space. The hypercube is a good trade-off between maximum distance between nodes, and number of physical connections.

The hypercube architecture is used by nCube, the Intel iWarp, and the Transputer. In each case, the basic processor chip has a communications capability built in. The Transputer and the iWarp have 4 high speed serial nodes each, and the nCube chip has 12, going to 16 for the nCube3. Thus, the Transputer and iWarp can each be directly connected in an Order-4 hypercube, and the nCube2 in an order 12.

The iWarp achieves a communication to computation

ratio of 1:1. Each iWarp component consists of an integer and a floating point computation section, and a communication element. The communication element supports 4 full duplex I/O channels, of 160 Mbytes/second input and output capability. Message passing exploits worm-hole routing for low overhead. Multiple logical connections on one physical channel is possible, similar to Inmos' virtual link concept. Fine grained, systolic communication is supported.

A crossbar switch may be used if the processor does not support sufficient interconnects. The Inmos C004 16x16 crossbar switch chip provides this function for the serial links of the Transputer. A crossbar switch functions like a telephone company central office, connecting any input to any output upon demand. The circuit remains for the duration of the message, or can be quasi-permanent. The latency introduced by the switch is minimal, about 1/2 bit time in the Inmos case. This is important where several switches must be traversed.

The nCube' machine's interconnection is via a hypercube topology. Each nCube2 has 13 I/O engines, one of which is used for I/O. Thus, an order 12 Hypercube is supported, or up to 4096 nodes. The worst case (longest distance) communication latency is on the order of the Hypercube, or 12, in the largest configuration. The nCube3 machine will use a new chip that will operate at 50 Mhz. Up to 65k processors can be included, since each processor chip includes 18 channels, 16 for the hypercube, and 2 for I/O. The channels now operate at

100mbps, due to use of 2 bit parallel (up from 1 bit, serial). nCubes's differentiator is its interconnection speed, at 2.5 megabytes/second bi-directional, with a factor of 10 improvement coming. The nCube-III will have dynamic routing, where each channel can support transfers at 20 Mbytes/second. There will be 18 communications channels on-chip, each 4 bits wide (2 in, 2 out). The channels will operate at 2x clock, 50 mbytes/second peak each, or 200 mbytes/second aggregate. The latency will be less than 2 microseconds, with 200 nanosecond internode forwarding. Adaptive routing will be used.

Tree

One variation of the tree architecture is the Fat Tree interconnect, favored by Meiko and by Thinking Machines for the CM-5 series. A key factor is whether the tree is 'pruned' or complete. What differentiates the CS-2 from the TMC CM-5 is that the CS-2 uses a complete tree interconnect, where the CM-5 uses a pruned tree. In theory, the CS-2 has a larger bisectional bandwidth as the system scales to larger numbers of nodes. The Meiko architecture supports up to 8 layers in the tree, giving a worst case path in a 256 node configuration of 7 switches. The maximum delay thru a tree architecture is on the order of the tree. Meiko's bisectional bandwidth scales to 102 Gbytes /second. There is an independent low bandwidth parallel bus for diagnostics and maintenance.

The interprocessor communications topology and chips are of Meiko's design. The Elan and ELITE chip are

82

made by Texas Instruments. The ELAN is the network interface processor on each compute node. It provides a coherent Mbus processor interface. The ELITE is the network switch processor, which is a 4x4 full crossbar. The ELITE achieves a 10 microsecond latency with a linear (scalable) bisection bandwidth. What differentiates the CS-2 from the TMC CM-5 (section 5.4.3) is that the CS-2 uses a complete tree interconnect, where the CM-5 uses a pruned tree. In theory, the CS-2 has a larger bisectional bandwidth as the system scales to larger numbers of nodes. The Meiko architecture supports up to eight layers in the tree, giving a worst case path in a 256 node configuration of 7 switches.

Each I/O connection of TMC's fat-tree interconnect provides a 20 Mbyte/second bisection bandwidth, that scales. Latency ranges from 3-7 microseconds. A separate control network is maintained, that supports broadcast and combining functions, and global synchronization. A diagnostic network uses JTAG and a special software diagnostics package. The TM-5 machine is scalable to 16,000 units.

Torus

The Torus arrangement is a 3-D structure, used by Tandem, Convex, and the Cray T3D. The T3D is scalable to hundreds or thousands of processors, using its sophisticated interconnect and memory system. It can support up to 2048 compute nodes, using a 3-D torus interconnection. The interconnect is bi-directional 2 bytes wide, and gives a peak transfer rate of 300 Mbps between nodes. The sustained bandwidth is about half that.

Transfers are directed, and packet switched. The T3D implements Cray's shared distributed memory scheme, in which any processor can address any memory in the system. The base Alpha processor's data translation look-aside buffer (D-TLB) has been extended to resolve memory address to the node where it resides. Each node hosts up to 64 Mbytes. A random read anywhere in the Torus interconnect can be satisfied within 1 microsecond.

The Convex Exemplar supports up to 128 processors, organized as hypernodes of up to 8 processors connected by a crossbar, of bandwidth 2.5 gigabytes/second. Interconnect latency is on the order of 100's of nanoseconds. Each hypernode has its own memory which is shared among the processors in the hypernode. A hypernode can be thought of as a tightly coupled, shared memory SMP. I/O interfaces are distributed across the hypernodes. A second level torroidal interconnect is used between hypernodes. This scalable toroidal interconnect (sci) is based on the IEEE Scalable Coherent Interface (IEEE 1596-1992), and provides 4 unidirectional rings with a capacity of up to 2 gigabytes per second. Sequential access to memory are interleaved across the rings of the toroid, for load balancing. The hypernode can be thought as a tightly coupled, fine-grained system, and the collection of hypernodes can be thought of as a coarse-grained, message-passing architecture. The overall machine has coherent distributed memory, and a large I/O system that is also distributed. Sixty four channels per I/O unit can be used, to a total of 4096 channels. The Service processor functionality is distributed among the hypernodes, with options for boot, diagnostics, and monitoring. JTAG is used for diagnostic scans of the hardware. A systems console (service hypernode) is used, with a separate and independent DaRT (diagnostic and testing bus), that operates in parallel with the interconnect busses.

Networking between nodes in the Tandem system takes one of several forms. For up to 16 cpu's, 4 gigabytes of memory, and 64 I/O channels, a TorusNet internal networking architecture is used. For up to 224 cpu's, 57 gigabytes of memory, and 896 I/O channels, a variation called the TorusNet Domain is used. For the high end system, the multi-domain TorusNet supports 4080 cpu's.

Reconfigurable topologies

All too often, a parallel program's efficiency depends on the communication topology. This means this factor must be considered by the programmer, and it makes the porting of code from a machine with one topology to another with a different topology very difficult. Topologies can be made configurable with cross-bar switches, or with virtual links.

Statically Reconfigurable Systems

In a statically reconfigurable system, the communications interconnect topology is pre-configured before run time for a schema that the systems analyst has selected. The communications system then remains in that format throughout the run. For example, the analyst could choose a ring, a torus, a hypercube, or a mesh.

Dynamically Reconfigurable Systems

In a dynamically reconfigurable system, the communications interconnect topology can be changed at run time. The implications of this are that, in case of error, you may not know the machine state, or the interconnect state. A much better set of debugging tools is needed for this class of machine.

The advantage of a dynamic reconfiguration capability is that it allows the machine itself to search for optimal communication topologies for given problem sets. This may take the form of searching in a solution space for the minimization of a particular cost function, usually associated with run time (time to solution). Metrics such as processor loading or communications link usage may be considered.

Shared Memory Systems

This section discusses systems with shared memories. Several approaches have been used.

Multiported memory

If we have 2 or 4 processors, we may connect these with a multiported memory. The memory would include the contention resolution mechanisms to arbitrate between processors attempting to access a single location simultaneously. Thus, the multiport mechanism built into the memory itself solves the contention problem (by a predetermined scheme, such as; "Port A always has priority").

The problem with this approach is that multiported memory (MPM) is expensive, of small capacity, and does not scale well beyond about 4 ports. This approach, however, has some merit, particularly if the processors and MPM can be combined onto one chip, or multichip module. The expensive problem is only because of economy of scale in manufacturing, as commodity DRAM is the cheapest memory in cost per bit of storage, because it is manufactured in the largest volume.

The next approach would be to have a very fast bus connecting processors with large caches to large memory modules. In fact, we could consider the memory as totally consisting of cache. This is KSR's approach.

In the KSR design, all of memory is treated as cache. A Harvard style, separate bus for instruction and memory is used. Each node board contains 256kbytes of I-cache and D-cache, essentially primary cache. At each node is 32 megabytes of memory for main cache. The system level architecture is shared virtual memory, which is physically distributed in the machine. The programmer or application only sees one contiguous address space, which is spanned by a 40 bit address. Traffic between nodes travels at up to 4 gigabytes per second. The 32 Megabytes per node, in aggregate, forms the physical memory of the machine.

KSR uses a ring architecture with 32 processors per ring on the KSR1, 64 processors in the KSR2. Scalability is achieved by interconnecting multiple rings via a hierarchical fat tree.

KSR implements a ring topology (toroidal). This topology has some interesting features. By coupling two rings by a high-speed WAN, systems could be geographically distributed but still appear to be a single computer.

Distributed Memory Systems

Looking at the communication problem from another angle, we may decide to tackle it not from a memory but from an I/O standpoint. In the distributed memory approach, we have a processor and memory at each node, and these nodes are connected by a communications network. Again, several options present themselves. We can use dedicated, point-point links. This scheme is limited in scalability by the number of links available, and the interfacing hardware. For example, the Transputer chip comes with 4 dedicated I/O links, each capable of 20 mbps per second each. At the node end, the links terminate in a dma engine that interfaces with the processor's memory. In the case of the Transputer, all of this is on one chip. Similarly, the proprietary chip used by nCube in their latest machine has 16 links for interprocessor communication. The iWarp chip has 4 channels, and the TMS series of RISC-DSP chips has 6. Most of these links are asynchronous serial, but the TI chip has parallel links, limiting the distance between processors. On the other hand, the parallel scheme is faster but distance limited. If you plan to pull it all onto one chip, as TI did with their TMS320C080 variant, it becomes awesomely fast, but connection-limited.

Distributed memory systems come with a "built-in" physical communication scheme between processors. On top of this, we need a communications and messaging protocol, interfaced with the operating system. One approach is the public domain software package PVM (Parallel Virtual Machine).

Speaking of operating systems, we can choose to implement the entire operating system at each node of the distributed memory system, but this uses up a lot of memory, particularly for Unix. Another approach is to have a kernel at each node, requiring several hundred kbytes, as opposed to 10's of Megabytes. Support for parallel distributed systems is emerging in several operating systems, notably for Windows-NT and OS-2.

In the distributed memory model, there is no requirement to have homogeneous systems. The distributed system resembles a network or a cluster of minicomputers more than one big homogeneous machine. Software such as PVM can link diverse systems across the communications network into one large worker.

Physical Interconnect

The interface between the computer backbone bus system and the secondary storage has a major influence on performance. The obvious parameter is the raw transfer speed from the disk drive electronics to the system memory. Of equal importance, however, is the number of control paths from the computer to the disk electronics, and from the drive controller to the drives. An extension of the RAID paradigm (discussed later) extends to multiple controller units for drives, extending to one controller per drive.

Interfaces to RAID type disk arrays in common use include SCSI, fast/wide SCSI, IDI, and ATA (enhanced IDE). The older MFM and RLL interfaces are now rarely used. These interfaces connect the disk drive(s) to a backplane bus. The HIPPI interface is also gaining favor for high performance applications.

Another concept, similar to a network printer, is to have network-attached storage. Here, the storage is stand-alone, and connected to a network, as opposed to being connected to a particular computer. We can think of these as storage servers or file servers, depending on the location of the metadata.

Transfer rates of Various SCSI Interfaces

	Mbytes/sec
SCSI-1	5
SCSI-2	
fast	10
wide	20
fast-wide	40
SCSI-3	>40

Fibre Channel

Fibre Channel is an industry-standard interface adopted by the American National Standards Institute. It is usually thought of as a system-to-system or system-to-subsystem interconnection architecture that uses optical cable between systems in a point-to-point (or switch) configuration. Fibre Channel is a generic, standard interface, and can support a variety of protocols, such as: SCSI, IPI-3,IP, and ATM.

A Fibre Channel loop supports data rates up to 100 MB/s (megabytes per second). Video storage and retrieval, supercomputer modeling, and image processing are among the applications growing in popularity that demand this kind of data rate. Moreover, as file servers are looked upon as replacements for mainframe computers, they will require ever-higher transaction rates to provide comparable levels of service. Since most UNIX and Windows servers lack the sophisticated I/O channel and controller structures of mainframe computers, they have not been able to match the large number of high-performance disc drives enterprise systems can support. Fibre Channel loops attached to such high-performance buses as S-Bus, Turbochannel or PCI-- all of which run 70 MB/s or faster--offer I/O configurations that can sustain mainframe-like I/O rates. Performance estimates suggest that if a system requests the relatively short I/O transfers typical of business transaction processing (8K or less), more than 60 drives can be supported without saturating the loop and bogging down performance. Comparing the single host adapter to the many channels and controllers mainframes employ to attach as many drives illustrates the remarkable economics of Fibre Channel-attached disc storage.

Since the Fibre Channel interface is part of the Fibre Channel standard, optical cabling can be used in any part of a subsystem, excluding the backplane. This makes it possible to have a disc subsystem quite a distance from the computer system to which it is attached. Using single-mode fibre optics, on-line disc storage could be as far as 10 km away. Fibre Channel makes Network Attached Storage architecturally practical.

In a typical non-fibre channel network the storage devices would be attached to a file server which would service the data needs of all other attached systems. The wide area network in diagram shows an FC loop with discs and systems attached. The systems could be communicating with the discs using SCSI and with each other using IP. Since the discs are directly attached to the same network as the systems there is no reason why all the systems could not communicate with the discs directly. All of the systems in the network could access the data at Fibre Channel speeds and avoid the file server bottleneck. These features are beneficial in a video server application where the data could be sent directly from the drive to a cable head or satellite at speeds much faster than any file server could move the data.

The memory speed needed to support 100 MB/s transfers concurrently with 20+ MB/s disc media transfer would have been a problem several years ago. The introduction of Cache DRAMS has made it possible to implement full 100 MB/s data/cache buffers for the same cost as supporting fast/wide SCSI.

SCSI-II

SCSI has become an interface of choice for medium- and large-sized computing systems. At the same time, the computer industry's experience with SCSI has brought to light the need for improvements in cable distance, number of variations, command overhead, array feature support and connectability.

SCSI comes in several different versions, but the majority of products shipping today are of the single-ended variety. (That is primarily because single-ended SCSIs cost less and are widely available.) If a SCSI bus is limited to connecting devices found within a single cabinet and the interface cable length does not exceed three meters, it usually is not a problem to use single-ended SCSI. If the bus must link several cabinets, however, and in the course of doing so must convert from an un-shielded ribbon cable in one cabinet to a shielded one externally, then back again to a ribbon cable within the second cabinet, the potential for SCSI signal problems increases. Differential SCSI solves this cabling issue, but usually requires that a system have both a single-ended and differential ports because most non-disc peripherals use only single-ended SCSI (single-ended SCSI devices cannot be attached to a differential bus).

New applications, like video and image processing have

created a demand for huge increases in storage capacity. Some capacity requirements are so large that it is difficult to configure enough SCSI buses to make sufficient drive addresses available to attach the needed number of drives. Simply increasing the addressability of SCSI, such as making it possible to have more than 15 devices per SCSI Wide bus, would not be a solution because more bus bandwidth is needed to support the additional drives.

SCSI's utility has improved with increased data rates several times since its introduction. Unfortunately, only the data rate has improved, which is the rate at which data is transferred off the disc. The rate at which SCSI interface information passes over a SCSI bus has not changed at all. SCSI command overhead is taking up an increasingly larger proportion of bus time, which makes it difficult to support multiple drives before the bus is saturated. Often peak transfer rate is achieved with three drives per each eight-bit bus, because three drives kept busy will produce so much SCSI protocol traffic that no additional drives can get any practical bandwidth that would contribute to the aggregate data rate.

Within the past few years, the computer industry has experienced a consolidation of disc drive interfaces. The ST412 interface once dominated the desktop, with MFM and RLL format drives accounting for the vast majority of disc drives sold. Other interfaces, such as ESDI, were predicted to have bright futures, but the market dictated otherwise. The handful of disc drive interfaces has since shrink down to two: ATA/IDE and the Small Computer Systems Interface (SCSI). As the performance needs of the desktop continue to grow, however, both of these interfaces have spawned a host of successors based on specific needs of the host platform. While ATA and its kin have had tremendous success in the PC market, the limitations of the ATA specification led users who were seeking higher performance and multiple device support to discover the benefits of SCSI. Just like in processors, disk drives have become commodity items, and the advantages of the economy of scale can't be ignored.

The SCSI has become the high performance standard for the computer industry. Featuring fast data transfer rates, a highly functional command set and the ability to support many devices on a single bus, SCSI offers an unparalleled combination of performance, flexibility and expand-ability. It is for these reasons that SCSI is used as a standard interface in computers ranging from the single user PCs through LAN servers and high performance RISC workstations, to MPMS supercomputers.

SCSI-2 was introduced a few years ago and added a host of new commands and functionality. These enhancements, which include caching, command queuing and power management, increased its performance and flexibility. The Fast-SCSI protocol then doubled the physical speed of the SCSI bus signals to allow faster data transfers and then Wide-SCSI specification doubled the width of the data path from eight bits to sixteen bits to allow even greater amounts of data to be transferred between SCSI devices and the host computer. The vast majority of SCSI drives currently sold for desktop machines implement Fast SCSI-2, while most modern workstations regularly support and use Fast Wide SCSI-2 devices.

Since SCSI is mainly used with multi-tasking operating systems, special demands were placed on the drive which often challenged the capabilities of standard drive architectures. Seagate Technology recognized that in order to create a true high performance drive, it was not enough to simply implement the particular requirements of a Fast or Wide SCSI version. The internal architecture of the drive itself must be designed to provide optimum performance in such demanding operating environments as UNIX, Windows95, Windows NT, Novell NetWare, or OS/2.

HIPPI

HIPPI refers to a high speed parallel interface. It is an ANSI standard for high speed I/O channels, defined for an 800 Mbps channel protocol. HIPPI spans the first and second layers of the OSI seven layer architecture. HIPPI's origin is with high speed host-to-host networking of supercomputers at the Los Alamos National Laboratory. HIPPI is a point to point, simplex connection.

The physical layer of HIPPI uses one hundred parallel copper wires, organized as fifty twisted pair, of maximum length 25 meters. Serial HIPPI refers to a fiber cable implementation, good to 10 kilometers. There are numerous commercial HIPPI products on the market.

ATM

ATM (Asynchronous Transfer Mode) is a cell switching technology applicable to LAN, WAN, and system interconnect. ATM uses a standard 53 byte cell, consisting of 5 bytes of header, and 48 bytes of payload. The payload can contain digitized data of any type: video, voice, image. ATM switches provide low latency, and ATM links are high speed. ATM scales from 51 Mbps to 1.2 Gbps and beyond.

Issues in Mass Storage

This section describes some of the issues in mass storage systems for massively parallel architectures. Unless systems with giga-ops/second capability are matched with commensurate storage systems in the gigabytes range, the systems are unbalanced.

This section will discuss the high performance mass storage systems required by the parallel processing machines to accomplish the data hosting tasks envisioned.

DASD

This section discusses the current state of the art in direct access storage devices (dasd). This includes rotating magnetic disks with non-removable media. Also included is a section on RAID technology -- Redundant Arrays of Inexpensive disks.

Rotating magnetic disk systems are random access, as opposed to the sequential nature of tape systems. There are multiple concentric tracks, as opposed to the single, spiral track of optical (CD-ROM) systems. Disk systems suffer from a long latency (compared to semiconductor memory), due to the motion of mechanical components.

Magnetic hard disc areal density is increasing at about 60% per year. Since bit density (measured in bits per inch), one of the two components of areal density, increases at about 30% per year, data rate automatically increases proportionately. Disc rotation speeds, which have doubled over the last five years from 3,600 to 7,200 as they continue to climb, also contribute to higher data rates. In the next few years drives will be introduced which can sustain transfers in excess of 20 MB/s, thanks solely to improvements in bit density and rotational speed. Disc drives in the market transfer data at rates over 10 MB/s.

Rotating magnetic media started out as adjuncts to mainframe computers. Interfaces and formats were customized, and non-interchangeable. Disk platter sizes ranged to five feet in diameter. An after market developed in supplying drives to fit with the few standard controllers, such as IBM or Univac. IBM introduced the first magnetic hard disk unit in 1956, a 24" unit. Current technology is predominately 1.8" platters. The key operational parameter of bits per unit area (areal density) for disk drives has been increasing at 60% per year since 1991. The current technology in read heads for magnetic disks, the Magneto-restrictive or MR head, flies two-millionths of an inch above the spinning disk surface. This is less than the wavelength of visible light. The MR head addresses the limiting performance of inductive-type heads, whereby the signal goes down as the bit packing density or data transfer rate goes up.

The explosive growth of the personal computer industry, coupled with a desire for constantly increasing amounts of online storage, drove the development of small, inexpensive disks. Starting out as 5 and 10 megabyte units with the shipment of the IBM XT model, these drives now exceed 2 gigabytes in capacity. The workstation and mainframe communities have adopted arrays of these inexpensive, mass-produced disks, according to the RAID paradigm, developed at U.C. Berkeley. The economies of scale are such that large arrays of mass-produced disks provide a better storage cost per dollar than custom units, with the additional benefit of providing layers of redundancy, error correction, and graceful degradation.

DASD pricing trends expressed in dollars per megabyte have show a decline from $7800 in 1956 to less than a dollar by 1994, a rate of decline of 15-20% per year. It is expected to accelerate to 25-35% per year. The equivalent price for tape systems is below $0.01 per megabyte. There is projected to be about 100 petabytes of installed disk storage by the end of calendar year 1996. The DASD market was at the level of $5 Billion in 1995.

Key parameters of any disk system include the seek time, overall latency, and transfer rate. The seek time is a function of the head positioning servo mechanism and rotational speed of the device. The seek time is the largest component of latency. A first approximation to the seek time is one-half of the rotational rate of the disk. Thus, within limits of strength of materials, a faster rotation rate is better. This also implies a faster data transfer rate. Apparent seek time can be reduced by large RAM-based track cache buffers on the disk controller itself. By the year 2000, rotation rates are expected to exceed 10,000 rpm, and data transfer rates to exceed 30 megabytes per second, with latencies below several milliseconds.

RAID

The idea of using inexpensive disks in redundant storage arrays was documented in Patterson, et al's paper in 1987. Generally, 5 levels of RAID are recognized. Instead of mapping files to a single actuator/head, RAID spreads these across heads and/or drives. This provides a gain in transfer rate, as well as providing for redundancy and error detection/correction. In addition, Arrays can provide hot-standby units, and hot-swap capability for drives. RAID addresses failures in drives, but not in the associated controllers. This may be addressed in future levels of the standard.

RAID is the growth area for disk drives, with RAID products currently addressing LAN and client/server workstation clusters, and scheduled to appear for detached workstations shortly. The development area within RAID will be for more intelligent controllers, using embedded RISC or DSP controllers, to enhance throughput, and reduce apparent latency. Redundant power supplies, backup power, and smart switch-over are also required for system-level data integrity. Other features of interest include dynamic sparing and spares management, and built-in maintenance and diagnostics.

RAID Levels

0   In this mode, data is striped across drives to maximize I/O   rate.   There   is   no   implementation of
     error detection or correction, or redundancy.
1   implements disk mirroring or shadowing. All data
is   duplicated for redundancy. Uses twice the
     physical storage.
2   Implements level 2, with error correction, usually a Hamming code.
3   Implements striping of records across all disks. Parity information goes to its own drive.
4   data interleaved to disks at sector level. As opposed to level 3 complete records are stored to a single disk. There is a dedicated parity drive. These units can only do one write, but multiple
     reads at a time.
5   Features striping by block size. Distributes data and parity   per sector across all drives.

Also defined is RAID level 6, in which two sections of each disk are set aside for parity information, and level 7, which uses asynchronous movement of drive heads, for improved write performance.

Mass Store

Two main questions must be answered. First, are the data capacities and transfer rates of the parallel processing machines commensurate with those of mainframes; and what is the projected size of the file structure / database?

Processor speeds have increased 1 to 2 orders of magnitude over the last few years while rotating magnetic media performance has increased by a factor of about 3. This is due to the limitations of the mechanical and servo positioning systems. Although magnetic media will dominate the non-volatile market in the near term, the performance increases to be expected are severely limited by the base technology. Optical media does not provide any magic answers, except in greater capacity.

The IEEE Mass Storage Systems Reference Model provides a standard for the implementation of Mass Storage Systems. It is currently in its fifth draft.
Backup

All online mass storage systems require some form of archival backup, not only to ensure against data loss, but also to limit the amount of on-line data storage. Near-line systems, such as tape silo systems, provide an intermediary capacity , and off-line systems provide archival facilities with longer latency, and longer retention. Common methods of backing up online magnetic storage is 9 track magnetic tape, tape cartridge or cassette, or worm (write-once, read many) optical media (disk or tape). The useful life of open reel tape is 10-15 years, with periodic respooling, and proper storage. The useful life of tape cartridge systems is also 10-15 years, with yearly rewinding and re-tentioning. The useful life of optical media is unknown, but estimated to be in excess of 100 years, under ideal storage conditions. Batelle Institute estimates the life of optical tape at 30 years.

The problem with any storage media is that either the drive/reader must be stored with the media to ensure readability when required, or the media must be transferred to newer media every 5 years or so. An example of this would be the transition from 8" to 5 1/4" to 3 1/2" floppy disk media.

Systems & Projects

This section discusses a series of commercial systems and projects involving the construction of Massively Parallel machines made from multiple commodity processors.

Transtech

Transtech, a company founded in 1986 and based in the U. K., builds systems from board level modules using the T-800 Transputer as the communication element, and the i860 as the compute element. They also developed a line of products around the TI TMS320C40 DSP processor, the PowerPC, and the Analog Devices SHARC. They also integrated the Inmos T-9000 chip, but the lateness of that chip's emergence cause quite a few market windows to be missed.

Up to 8 SHARC processors are hosted on a PCI, ISA, or VME card. The communications architecture of the SHARC processor means that transputers need not be used to implement communications between compute nodes. Similarly, the TI C040 based products do not need auxiliary help with inter-processor communication.

The PowerPC modules form Transtech use the 603 or 604 processors on PCI or VME boards, with a T-805 transputer for communication. Similarly, the I860 products use the T-805 in a communications role.

Meiko

Meiko is better known as a U.K. based, European parallel processing vendor, but does have a presence in US applications. Their earlier approach was to use the Transputer T-800 chip as a communication agent, with the i860 as a computer engine, augmented by Fujitsu vector processors. This was the Computing Surface (CS-1) machine, of which several hundred were sold. The Inmos Transputer architecture, introduced in 1985, is a single chip microcomputer architecture, optimized for parallel use in Multiple Instruction, Multiple Data (MIMD) configurations. It provided balanced interprocessor communications as well as computational ability. Meiko re-engineered the machine into the CS-2 model, which is based on the SPARC merchant RISC chip. Meiko is the Japanese word for "well-engineered".

Meiko is one of the pioneers of scalable systems constructed from commodity microprocessors. Meiko considers their most notable achievement to be a >800 cpu system at the Lawrence Livermore National Laboratory in California. Meiko is legally an American company. Meiko has sold many large systems around the world - except, curiously, in the UK - and now focuses on the rapidly growing server markets, especially those for data warehousing using Oracle, and the Internet.

The basic Meiko machine supports up to 256 processors per module, with multiple modules connected by switches into large systems. Each processor module has its own memory and I/O resources. A processing element includes the SPARC cpu, a communications processor, and up to 512 Mbytes of memory. Two variations on the basic processor provide either an Ethernet connection, two SCSI fast/wide ports, and three S-bus ports, or 4 processors on a card. Nodes can incorporate specialized vector processors from Fujitsu. Meiko estimates that it would take them 6 month to change hardware architectures, based on past experience of the change from the Transputer to the SPARC. They are not locked into the SPARC processor.

The CS-2 machine runs the Solaris 2.3 operating system, with a complete version at each node. It has been augmented with unique device drivers for the interprocessor communications network, and parallelization tools. This provides a migration path for Solaris applications. One software application is PANDORA, which gives the user system partition and global views of applications. Standard industry I/O interfaces such as HIPPI, FDDI, ATM, Fibrechannel, and ethernet are supported. SCSI-interfaced disks are used.

There were 6 original founders of Meiko in 1985, of whom 5 were engineers from Inmos, and were original developers of the Transputer chip. Meiko is an employee-owner company. Outside investment will allow them to invest in the commercial market. Meiko concentrates on the high end of the market - MPP, not scaled-up SMP. Meiko's marketing approach is described as "stealth" by Gartner Group. Meiko has a large presence in Europe, especially with systems running Oracle. The Meiko

107

machine is a cornerstone in the lab's plan to replace traditional Cray-class supercomputers with parallel machines. The lab machine is being built at the Meiko facility in Concord, MA.

The inter-processor communications topology and chips are of their design. The Elan and ELite chip are made by Texas Instruments. The ELAN is the network interface processor on each compute node. It provides a coherent Mbus processor interface. The ELITE is the network switch processor, which is a 4x4 full crossbar. They achieve a 10 microsecond latency, with a linear (scalable) bisection bandwidth.

What differentiates the CS-2 from the TMC CM-5 is that the CS-2 uses a complete tree interconnect, where the CM-5 uses a pruned tree. In theory, the CS-2 has a larger bisectional bandwidth as the system scales to larger numbers of nodes. The Meiko architecture supports up to 8 layers in the tree, giving a worst case path in a 256 node configuration of 7 switches. The bisectional bandwidth scales to 102 Gbytes/second. There is an independent low bandwidth parallel bus for diagnostics and maintenance.

Intel SSD

Intel Corporation has done several projects in massively parallel systems. As a chip vendor, Intel has an interest in developing a market for machines that use multiple copies of its chips. Some have been one-of-a-kind research machines, funded by the defense establishment during the Cold War period. The Paragon series address the commercial marketplace, as well as the traditional scientific/engineering community. First based on the i860 chip, later models incorporated the Pentium, chip or subsequent, and Intel's development of the 64 bit successor to the i860 has been dropped.

Another totally different approach from Intel was the iWarp processor. It derived from H.T. Kung's work at Carnegie Mellon University, and the earlier CMMP and CM* projects. It found limited interest outside of DARPA applications. The iWarp is discussed in a separate section.

The Paragon series of machines from Intel Supercomputer Systems Division (SSD) used the i860XP chips, running OSF/1 UNIX. It is a successor to the earlier iPSC/860 series. Parallelizing compilers for C and FORTRAN are available.

Intel's "Touchstone Delta" System was a one-of-a-kind system built for the California Institute of Technology, using 520 of the i860 processor chips.

The iPSC series used up to 128 of the 40 Mhz i860 chips. A shared I/O design, special I/O nodes based on the i80386 were used. These used a SCSI interface, TCP/IP support, and a VME board interface. The internal networked, called 'Direct-Connect', provided bidirectional 5.6 Mbyte/second channels in a switched configuration. A Unix-based kernel called NX/2 resided at each node, and a Unix model Concurrent file system was supported. Parallel CASE tools were available for Fortran and c. Network Queuing System (NQS) is supported. The interactive parallel debugger (ipd) and parallel performance analysis tools (pat) were also developed for this system.

The Paragon machine scales to 1024 of the i860XP processors, arranged in SMP type, 4 processor nodes. Each node can have up to 128 Mbytes of memory. An I/O type node can be added to support interfaces such as HIPPI, FDDI, ethernet, and ultranet. The inter-processor communication architecture scales as nodes are added. A 2D mesh configuration, with a mesh router for each node, provides a message passing architecture with a bidirectional node-node bandwidth of 200 Mbytes per second, and a latency of 40 Nanoseconds per node hop. The operating system is OSF/1, with a Mach 3.0 micro-kernel at each node. File system services are provided from special service nodes. Fortran and c are supported, along with optimized libraries, performance monitoring, and debugging tools. Paragon systems are installed at many National laboratories, and Intel sold 50 in 1993. Commercial users such as Prudential Securities are using them as well.

Intel's future directions in massively parallel computing is defined with collections of PentiumPro chips or their successors, as there has been no recent development work on the iWarp or i860 architecture. Intel will concentrate on the Pentium successors, and the commoditization of interconnect (the iMRC chip). They have partnered with Unisys in the commercial field. They have a Video server project with Microsoft. They have partnered with Honeywell for MIL systems. They view the Paragon, and successors, not as a supercomputer replacement, but as a general purpose server. They see the technical computing market place as the technology driver; the commercial marketplace as the market driver. In the commercial world, Intel developments will probably be brought to market by Unisys and other Intel commercial partners.

Mercury Computer Systems

Mercury Computer Systems address the real-time market with board and box level products that have the throughput of supercomputer systems. The target applications are signal and image processing, and classical DSP-type applications. They make use of the i860, the PowerPC, and the SHARC processor architectures. Their processor interconnect is the RACEway backplane bus system.

Sky Computers

Sky Computers makes a line of VME add-in boards using the i960 as a communication element, and multiple TMS320c0x0, i860, or SHARC chips for processors.

NCube

nCube is based on a proprietary chip design, currently 32 bits, going to 64 bits. This chip is currently fabricated by HP. A single chip plus DRAM chips makes a module, which are combined on boards into systems. The advantage of nCube's approach is minimization of components; all necessary logic is built onto the single chip. A node is made up of the processor chip, plus DRAM. No other components are required. The current generation machine is the nCube 2. The nCube 2S uses a newer and faster processor.

Each chip runs a 200 kbyte microkernel (nCX), although the box and associated front end (SUN/SGI) runs a Unix-derived Parallel Software Environment (PSE). A "single wide" module holds 16 megabytes, with a "double wide" module holding 32 megabytes. The I/O subsystem uses the same modules, with different backend interfaces to support SCSI, and other popular interfaces. Up to 96-way disk striping is supported, and has been tested.

Interconnection is via a hypercube topology. Each nCube2 has 13 I/O engines, one of which is used for I/O. Thus, an order 12 Hypercube is supported, or up to 4096 nodes. The worst case (longest distance) communication latency is on the order of the Hypercube, or 12, in the largest configuration.

The nCube3 machine will use a new chip that will operate at 50 Mhz, and achieve almost single cycle operation, even for the floating point operations. Data and Instruction cache is included. Up to 65k processors can be included, since each processor chip includes 18 channels, 16 for the hypercube, and 2 for I/O. The channels now operate at 100mbps, due to use of 2 bit parallel (up from 1 bit, serial).

nCube is one of the few MPP vendors that do not use merchant processor chips. nCube is also closely aligned with Oracle Corp. to address the parallel relational database and video server markets.

nCubes's differentiater is its interconnection speed, at 2.5 megabytes/second bidirectional, with a factor of 10 improvement coming. There are currently 14 I/O paths per node. The nCube-III will have 18 paths, and dynamic routing.

The nCube-III chip will feature a 64 bit ALU, and be superscalar. It will initially operate at 50 Mhz, going to 66 and 100. It targets 50 mips and 100 mflops at 50 mHz. It will have a 16kbyte I-cache, and a 16kbyte D-cache, with virtual memory support, and some new instructions. There will be 18 communications channels onchip, each 4 bits wide (2 in, 2 out). The channels will operate at 2x clock, or 50 megabytes/second peak each, 200 mbytes/second aggregate. The latency will be less than 2 microseconds, with 200 nS internode forwarding. Adaptive routing will be used. Memory will be up to 1 gigabyte of synchronous DRAM, with a 800 mbytes/second bandwidth. The nCube node has only the cpu and memory, no glue logic, because of the integrated design of the chip. The pci bus will be used.

nCube's hardware engineering and manufacturing are in Beverton, Or. They use a full custom VLSI approach, which drives the cost down. The nCube-III chips will use 0.5 micron, 3 level metal CMOS, operating at 3.3 volts, and utilizing 3.26 million transistors. Thus, nCube is not that far behind the merchant chip power curve. They do their design and simulation on nCube machines. They feature low latency channels and balanced I/O. The nCube-II chips operate at 25 Mhz, with the nCube-III going to 50 Mhz. Each node runs a 100k byte microkernel, not the entire operating system.

The nCube-III will use up to 65k processors to achieve 3 million MIPS, and 6.5 teraflops. The maximum memory will be 65 terabytes, with an aggregate network I/O capability of 24 Terabytes/second. Thus, the processor is biased in terms of I/O, which is usually the limitation. The nChannel board provides 16 I/O channels, where each channel can support transfers at 20 Mbytes/second.

The nCube 2E series is an entry-level, deskside machine with 8-128 processors. It features up to 4 gigabytes of main memory, and up to 64 I/O channels. The 2 and 2S can scale to 8192 processors, and each supports SCSI, HIPPI, and ethernet. The c and c++ languages are available, as is NQS, Linda, and Parasoft's Express.

The nCube machine is based on a proprietary chip design, currently 32 bits (the nCUBE2) , going to 64 bits (nCUBE3). This chip is currently fabricated by HP. A single chip plus DRAM chips makes a module, which are combined on boards into systems. The advantage of nCube's approach is minimization of components; all

114

necessary logic is built onto the single chip. This is similar to the Transputer T-800 and iWarp, but with more I/O channels. A "single wide" module holds 16 megabytes, with a double wide module holding 32 megabytes. The I/O subsystem uses the same modules, with different backend interfaces to support SCSI, etc. A node supports to 16 megabytes of memory on a board about 1" x 3.5". Up to 64 megabytes are available on a double side board.

Interconnection is via hypercube. Each nCube2 has 13 I/O engines, one of which is used for I/O. Thus, an order 12 Hypercube is supported, or up to 4096 nodes. The worst case (longest distance) communication is the order of the Hypercube, or 12 in this case.

The nCUBE3 is a new chip that will operate at 50 Mhz, and achieve near single cycle operation, even for the floating point operations. Data and Instruction cache is included. Up to 65k processors are included, since each processor chip includes 18 channels, 16 for the hypercube, and 2 for I/O. The channels now operate at 100mbps, due to use of 2 bit parallel (up from 1 bit, serial).

NCube has their own in-house compiler group, and tool developers. Each chip runs a 200 kbyte microkernel (nCX), although the box and associated front end (SUN/SGI) runs Unix. Full 64 bit IEEE floating point is supported.

Tera Computer

Tera Computer, not to be confused with Teradata, has designed and built a multi-threaded architecture with 16-256 custom processors in a shared memory configuration. It is Unix based, and extensive software simulation has taken place. Tera has been supported by DARPA. Chief architect was the world-famous Burton Smith.

Maspar

Maspar offered a family of SIMD machines, second sourced by DEC. The processor units are proprietary. MasPar existed the hardware business in June of 1996. The new software company was called NeoVista. There were over 250 MP-2 installations. There was no MP-3.

Each chip runs a 200 kbyte microkernel (nCX), although the box and associated front end (SUN/SGI) runs Unix. Is this POSIX compliant? A "single wide module holds 16 megabytes, with a double wide module holding 32 megabytes. The I/O subsystem uses the same modules, with different backend interfaces to support SCSI, etc. Up to 96-way disk striping is supported, and has been tested.

Interconnection is via hypercube. Each nCube2 has 13 I/O engines, one of which is used for I/O. Thus, an order 12 Hypercube is supported, or up to 4096 nodes. The worst case (longest distance) communication is the order of the Hypercube, or 12, here.

The nCube3 machine uses a new chip that will operate at 50 Mhz, and achieve almost single cycle operation, even for the floating point operations. Data and Instruction cache is included. Up to 65k processors are included, since each processor chip includes 18 channels, 16 for the hypercube, and 2 for I/O. The channels now operate at 100mbps, due to use of 2 bit parallel (up from1 bit, serial).

MasPar is unique in being a manufacturer of SIMD machines. In this approach, a collection of ALU's listen to a program broadcast from a central source. The ALU's can do their own data fetch, but are all under control of a central Array Control Unit. There is a central clock. The emphasis is on communications efficiency, and low latency. The MasPar architecture is designed to scale, and balance processing, memory, and communication.

Maspar uses a full custom CMOS chip, the MP-2 PE, designed in-house, and fabricated by various vendors such as HP or TI.

The Array Control Unit (ACU) handles instruction fetch. It is a load/store architecture. The MasPar architecture is Harvard in a broad sense. The ACU implements a microcoded instruction fetch, but achieves a RISC-like 1 instruction per clock. The Arithmetic units, ALU's with data fetch capability, are implemented 32 to a chip. Each ALU is connected in a nearest neighbor fashion to 8 others. The edge connections are brought off-chip. In this scheme, the perimeters can be toroid-wrapped. Up to 16,

384 units can be connected within the confines of a cabinet. A global router, essentially a cross-bar switch, provides external I/O to the processor array.

The MP-2 PE chip contains 32 processor elements, each a full 32 bit ALU with floating point, registers, and a barrel shifter. Only the instruction fetch feature is removed, and placed in the ACU. The PE design is literally replicated 32 times on the chip. The chip is designed to interface to DRAM, to other processor array chips, and to communication router chips.

Each ALU, called a PE slice, contains 64, 32-bit registers that are used for both integer and floating point. The registers are, interestingly, bit and byte addressable. The floating point unit handles single and double precision arithmetic on IEEE format numbers. Each PE slice contains two registers for data memory address, and the data. Each PE also has two bit serial ports, one for inbound and one for outbound communication for nearest neighbor. The direction of communication is controlled globally. The PE's also have inbound and outbound paths to a global router for I/O. A broadcast port allows a single instance of data to be "promoted" to parallel data. Alternately, global data can be 'or-ed' (demoted?) to a scalar result.

The serial links support 1 megabyte/second bit-serial communication that allows coordinated register-register communication between processors. Each processor has its own local memory, implemented in DRAM. No internal memory is included on the processors. Micro-coded instruction decode is used.

The 32 PE's on a chip are clustered into two groups sharing a common memory interface, or M-machine, for access. A global scoreboard keeps track of memory and register usage. The path to memory is 16 bits wide. Both big and little endian formats are supported. Each processor has its own 64kbytes of memory. Both direct and indirect data memory addressing are supported.

The chip is implemented in 1. micron two level metal CMOS, dissipates 0.8 watt, and is packaged in a 208 pin PQFP. A relatively low clock rate of 12.5 Mhz is used.

The Maspar machines are front ended by a host machine, usually a Vax. They are accessed by extensions to Fortran and C. Full IEEE single and double precision floating point are supported.

There is no cache for the ALU's. Cache is not required, due to the memory interface operating at commensurate speed with the alu data accesses.

The ALU's do not implement memory management for data memory. The ACU uses demand paged virtual memory for the instruction memory.

Pyramid

The Pyramid Technologies' SMP systems are extensions of the uniprocessors currently available. The NILE series

119

is SMP. The MESHine is MPP. Pyramid is a subsidiary of Siemens-Nixdorf.

The NILE machine hardware and software uses the R4400 chip, and provides up to a 24 node SMP. For massively scalable systems (their term) they use SMP's as the nodes in clusters. The keys to the technology as they see it are strategic relationships. The Nile series currently supports c/c++, Micro-focus Cobol, Informix, Sybase, and Oracle 7. The R-bus (derived from Future-bus) achieves 400 mbytes/second using 64 byte block transfers. It has 24 slots, is 128 bits (data) wide, and operates at 25 Mhz. The I/O bus is 32 bits wide, and operates at 40 Mbps.

The Nile series is scalable in processing power, I/O, and storage. Up to four gigabytes per processor node is available. Supported interfaces include SCSI-2, NFS, FDDI, and Ethernet. The operating system is the SMP version of Unix SVR4. The architecture is distributed memory, shared I/O. Pyramid has a defined path to doubling processing power every 12-18 months, while keeping I/O capabilities and storage capabilities commensurate.

The Mesh architecture, and the MESHine, was scheduled for a 1/95 introduction. One machine is already in place at Oracle. It is a shared-nothing design, using R4400 technology, commercial MPP. Mesh is a Cal Tech interconnect I/O design. This technique is also used in the Intel Paragon, and by Unisys. The links operate at 50 megabytes/second. One chip, of their own design, is the MRC, mesh router component, with 8-way, bidirectional connectivity. 4 kbyte messages are used, with an asynchronous protocol. The MESH has a full operating system at each node. It is designed as a data warehouse engine.

DEC

Digital Equipment Corporation (DEC) had taken many approaches to parallelism. They had at one time an agreement with Intel to resell the iPSC line, but that relationship has been terminated. DEC also resold MasPar's SIMD machines with a Vax front end. DEC's own efforts revolve around shared memory, SMP versions of machines based on DEC's own Alpha chip. DEC had extensive experience in clustering workstations and mid-range machines.

DEC was integrating multiple copies of their EV4 Alpha microprocessors into Alpha farms/clusters, using a shared memory architecture. The EV4 processor is a 64 bit RISC architecture, currently available at an operating speed of 500 Megahertz.

According to DEC, the Alpha architecture is designed for a twenty five year life, which represents eons in the RISC world, where the design life of a part may only be 18 months. The Alpha is a 64 bit superscalar, superpipelined architecture that was designed to provide viability for the minicomputer manufacturer into the next century. Besides longevity and high performance, the architecture is supposed to support easy migration from existing architectures, and to support multiple operating systems, including Unix (OSF - 64 bit) and Windows/NT.

DEC wass predominately a minicomputer company that has built up an understanding of software, users, systems, and networks over the years. It has a large installed base of machines in many different application areas, and a loyal cadre of users. DEC understands the computer business, not just the chip business. The company can build world class chips, as well as integrate those chips into boxes, and add software to be able to ship systems and solutions to end-users. DEC is saddled with the burden of the legacy Vax /VMS systems that represented it flagship line of minicomputers for years.

The Alpha machines were targeted to the desktop, and the department. By supporting industry standard multiplatform operating environments such as Windows/NT, DEC hopes to broaden the appeal of the product line, and open up access to existing software. At the same time, DEC will continue to provide support to the Unix and Vax worlds. Dec also hopes to build up a merchant chip business with Alpha chips (see Cray T3D).

At the Box level, the Sable SMP contains 4 cpu's sharing memory on a 667 megabytes /second, 128 bit wide bus. It is scalable to 12 cpu's, and to 2 cpu's per board. Nodes have their own local memory and I/O resources. Up to 512 megabytes of memory per node are currently available. Currently, the high end product contains 32 nodes.

Within a box, nodes are connected by the PCI bus at 132 megabytes/second in 32-bit wide mode, or 264 megabytes in 64-bit wide mode. Reflective memory techniques, developed by Encore Computer are used for shared memory-based clustering, via a PCI-PCI technique. Box interconnect is by Ethernet, FDDI @ 100 mbps, or Gigaswitch at 250 mbps. Giga-switch connects up to 22 FDDI ports via a crossbar mechanism.

Certain parallel tools and languages, previously available for other architectures, are being ported to the Alpha, including OSF 64 bit Unix based on the MACH kernel from Carnegie-Mellon University, PVM, Message Passing Protocol (MPP), and Network Linda, from Scientific Computing Associates. The Load Sharing Facility (LSF) software links Alphas and other Unix boxes into a heterogeneous cluster. The Parasoft Express operating system is also available. Express provides parallel I/O, library extensions to the c language, and debugging facilities. DEC is now owned by Compaq Computer.

Cray T3D/E

The Cray T3D uses multiple copies of DEC's Alpha 64 bit micro-processor. A system has been delivered to the Pittsburgh Supercomputing Center. The Cray MPP is an adjunct to the big Cray machines, and uses them as a front end. The T3D needs a Cray Y-MP or C90 as a front end. The follow-on T-3E generation is also not stand-alone. Cray has few commercial (non-number-crunching) customers. Cray is not doing much with commercial data bases, focusing on traditional high end engineering problems of the Grand Challenge class. This section does not discuss the traditional Cray high end vector supercomputers such as the Y-MP or EL90 series.

The T3D is scalable to hundreds or thousands of processors, using a sophisticated interconnect and memory system. It can support up to 2048 compute nodes, using a 3-D torus interconnection. The interconnect is bidirectional, 2 bytes wide, and gives a peak transfer rate of 300 Mbps between nodes. The sustained bandwidth is about half that. Transfers are directed, and packet switched.

The T3D implements Cray's shared distributed memory scheme, in which any processor can address any memory in the system. Alpha's data translation look-aside buffer (D-TLB) has been extended to resolve memory address to the node where it resides. Each node hosts up to 64 Mbytes. A random read anywhere in the Torus interconnect can be satisfied within 1 microsecond. I/O nodes use the Cray I/O subsystem design, and some I/O is handled by the supercomputer host.

The T3D runs a full version of the Unicos operating system at each node. Multi-threading is being implemented into Unicos. PVM and the c language are supported. Most Cray applications port easily to the T3D.

Cray is not married to the use of the Alpha architecture. The need to host the T3D with a traditional Cray Supercomputer limits its usefulness. The applicable of this machine to traditional business activities is not seen. Business computing activities are usually not floating point intensive, but rather involve very large database activities. These have not yet been addressed on the T3D. Some niche activities, such as statistics calculations, do require floating point performance, but these are in the minority. Several Cray T3D systems have been delivered to customer sites.

The T3E, introduced in 1996, uses the DEC Alpha EV5.6 chip clocked at 450 MHz.

NEC

NEC put together a MPP from MIPS R4000 processors. This is not available outside of Japan, as it runs a Japanese language version of Unix. Japanese MPMS are discussed in an appendix .

KSR

Kendall Square Research (KSR) of Waltham, Massachusetts, was founded in 1986. The company manufactured the KSR1 and KSR2 general-purpose, highly parallel MPPs using their patented Allcache memory system.

The Kendall Square Research machine used proprietary 64 bit processors in a large array to address high end applications. Offerings included the KSR-1 and KSR-2.

Besides the traditional scientific applications, KSR, in conjunction with ORACLE, addressed the massively parallel database market for commercial applications. The KSR-1 and -2 supported Microfocus COBOL and c/c++, as well as the Oracle PRDBMS and the MATISSE OODBMS from ADB, Inc. Their own product, the KSR Query Decomposer, complemented the functionality of the Oracle product for SQL uses. The TUXEDO transaction monitor for OLTP was also provided. The KAP program provided for pre-processing for source code analysis and parallelization.

Kendall Square Research's machines were based on their own chip design. The KSR-1 chipset was fabricated by Sharp, with the KSR-2 chipset being built by HP. The processor, implemented as a chipset, achieved two operations per cycle. Instruction decode was hardwired, and pipelining was used. Up to 1088 processor units could be constructed in the KSR-1. The KSR-2, also using the proprietary processors, scaled to over 5,000 processors.

The KSR-1 processor was implemented as a 4-chip set in 1.2 micron CMOS. These chips were: the Cell Execution Unit, the floating point unit, the integer and logical operations unit, and the external I/O unit (XIO). The CEU handled instruction fetch (2 per clock), and all operations involving memory, such as loads and stores. 40 bit addresses were used, going to full 64 bit addresses later. The integer unit had 32, 64 bit wide registers. The floating point unit is discussed below. The XIO had the capability of 30 Megabytes/second to I/O devices. It included 64 control and data registers.

KSR instructions were of 6 types: memory reference (load & store), execute, control flow, memory control, I/O, and inserted. Execute instructions included arithmetic, logical, and type conversion. They were usually triadic register in format. Control flow refers to branches and jumps. Branch instructions were two cycles. The programmer (or compiler) could implicitly control the "quashing" behavior of the subsequent two instructions that would be initiated during the branch. The choices were: always retain the results, retain results if branch test is true, or retain results if branch test is false. Memory control provided synchronization primitives. I/O instructions were provided. Inserted instructions were forced into a flow by a coprocessor. Inserted load and store were used for DMA transfers. Inserted memory instructions were used to maintain cache coherency. New coprocessors could be interfaced with the inserted instruction mechanism. IEEE standard floating point arithmetic was supported. Sixty-four 64-bit wide registers were included.

In the KSR design, all of the memory was treated as cache. A Harvard style, separate bus for instruction and memory was used. Each node board contained 256 kbytes of I-cache and D-cache, essentially primary cache. At each node was 32 megabytes of memory for main cache. The system level architecture was shared virtual memory, which was physically distributed in the machine. The programmer or application only saw one contiguous address space, which was spanned by a 40 bit address. Traffic between nodes traveled at up to 4 gigabytes per second. The 32 Megabytes per node, in aggregate, formed the physical memory of the machine.

Specialized I/O processors could be used in the system, providing scalable I/O. A 1088 node KSR1 could have 510 I/O channels with an aggregate in excess of 15 Gigabytes/second. Interfaces such as ethernet, FDDI, and HIPPI were supported. The system software was KSR OS, compatible with Unix, OSF/1, Posix, and X/Open. The runtime environment was termed PRESTO, and was a POSIX compliant multithreading manager.

KSR refocused its efforts from the scientific to the commercial marketplace, with emphasis on parallel relational databases and OLTP operations. It then got out of the hardware business, but continued to market some of its data warehousing and analysis software products.

Parsytec

Parsytec was very active in the European Teraflop Initiative, and initially put their bets on the Inmos T-9000 chip. With that chip delayed, they changed their focus to the PowerPC (IBM, Apple, Motorola). They use the T-800 Transputer as a communication agent. They have shipped systems in the US and Europe.

Thinking Machines Corp

The Connection Machine - 5 (CM-5) used the SPARC

128

microprocessor interconnected in a "fat tree" to provide a MIMD architecture. TMC's architecture is very like the Meiko machine. TMC addressed the commercial video server market, and numerous commercial database and data mining applications. The previous generation of the Thinking Machine (CM-1, CM-2) was SIMD, but the next generation was solidly MIMD. Thinking Machines was a pioneer in software tools development, and their tools take full advantage of the parallel architecture of their machine. The 'DARWIN' toolset provides a series of tools for data mining of very large data bases. TMC has been a pioneer in this area. The Oracle 7.1 Parallel RDBMS was also supported.

TMC's approach was to leverage commodity components (buy, not build), and weave these together into systems. Components used included commodity RISC microprocessors, memory, and SCSI-II disks. TMC considered that the hardware doesn't matter. TMC had the ability to transition to alternate architectures; they've did it before. They used SPARC, because they thought it had the best Unix (Solaris) at the time. It was augmented by TMC, and extended for large files (>32 bit addressing). The result was the operating system CMost. Partitioning the machine into different user and program areas was supported.

Along with the SPARC processors at each node, specialized vector processors were included. These were conneced to the SPARC, and provided Cray-type vector processing for the node. Each vector processor had its own set of 128, 32-bit wide registers. Each SPARC can keep up to 4 vector processors fed.

On the CM-5, control processors, also SPARC based, took care of I/O. They could also be used for partition management. I/O interfaces included Ethernet, and FDDI. A HIPPI interface could be added to the data network, and utilized 8 network interfaces.

Each I/O connection of the fat-tree interconnect provided a 20 Mbyte/second bisection bandwidth, that scaled. Latency ranged from 3-7 microseconds. A separate control network was maintained, that supported broadcast and combining functions, and global synchronization. A diagnostic network used JTAG and a special software diagnostics package.

The TM-5 machine was scale-able to 16,000 units. Los Alamos National Lab has 1500 units installed. The CM-5E used the faster SuperSPARC processors, faster vector units, and a faster network interface. CM-5E nodes can be retrofitted into an existing CM-5 machine.

TMC enjoyed sales into the commercial marketplace, such as American Express Co., Dow Jones, and Citibank. Non-defense, U.S. Government users included the U.S. Census Bureau, HHS (Medicare), and NASA. TMC got out of the hardware business, to focus on their software tools for data analysis.

Cray Superservers

Cray's Superservers are high end SMP machines that are Sun workstation compatible. They address the top end of Sun line, or the bottom end of the Cray line (both markets). They run an extended Solaris operating system, and the Oracle, Sybase, and Informix RDBMSs. They are Cray-MPP compatible at the source code level. The SuperServers can have 64 each of Processor Elements, memory, and I/O. Support for HIPPI, SCSI, Ethernet, and FDDI is included. Up to 16 gigabytes of memory and 64 channels of I/O are available. A standard S-bus is used for I/O interfaces.

The Cray Research 6400 server uses multiple TI SuperSPARC chips. The Superserver division of Cray was derived from the acquisition by Cray of Floating Point Systems. Unix (Solaris) is the operating system, extended to support some Unicos features such as networking. The Kerboros security feature is available.

The CS6400 system has demonstrated a scalability of 28 for a 32 node system. The system interconnect for the shared-nothing approach is 4 fast packet-switched XD buses. The console, or System Service Processor, is a Sun Workstation, and provides JTAG diagnostics for the system, besides administration and boot. N+1 redundancy is used for all modules.

A CS6400 system can be partitioned in software into independent processor sets. Software tools include the compilers for c and c++ as well as a Cray 90 development and Cray's version of PVM. OOPS and CASE tools are available, as generally is any software that runs under Solaris. Client and server modules for Cray's Network Queuing Environment are available, with support for load balancing across the machine.

Cray Superservers leveraged Cray Research, CraySoft, and Sun Microsystems resources to develop an integrated (hardware plus software) solution to commercial business problems.

IBM

IBM's SP-1 (Scalable Power-Parallel System) is an upper-end extension of their RS/6000 architecture. Up to 64 nodes are supported. The SP-1 series used the proprietary RIOS-I chipset. The SP-2 uses the new RIOS-II chip in a similar architecture. IBM expects to support 256 nodes or more in this series. SP-3, currently called SP-x, will ship in 1995/96, and use the PowerPC-620. All of the Power systems are currently SMP. The initial PowerPC chips are RIOS compatible.

IBM's POWER (Performance Optimization with Enhanced RISC) architecture defines a family of desktop and deskside machines with a wide spectrum of performance. The MCA bus is used. The operating system is AIX. The current generation chipset, introduced in 1990, is referred to as RIOS I, with a RIOS II being introduced in 1993. The high end RIOS-I can maximally execute 5 instructions per clock, going to 8 per clock in RIOS II. (2 branch, 2 integer, 2 floating point add, 2 floating point multiply)

The Power processor is a proprietary IBM design. Separate integer and floating point units operate simultaneously on-chip. Separate instruction and data caches are provided, as well as a branch processor, which can provide zero-cycle branches. 184 instructions are included in the set. The processor is capable of executing 4 instructions per clock. These have to be: one integer, one floating point, one branch, and one condition register operation.

The PowerPC family is a joint effort between IBM, Apple, and Motorola to design and manufacture a family of RISC processors scalable from palmtop to mainframe. The first in the series, the Motorola produced MC98601, is a 32 bit implementation of the 64 bit family architecture. First silicon appeared in 1992. The PowerPC design is a blend of IBM's RIOS processor architecture, and Motorola's 88100 internal bussing. IBM and Apple laid out the basic architecture of the device in 1991. The 601, first in the series, is a subset of the reference PowerPC architecture, and is 3 issue.

The PowerPC family includes the 601 processor, 603, 604, and 620. The 620 is a 64 bit architecture. The Power-PC design was influenced by the previous ROMPS architecture. n dynamically order load/store memory traffic at run time, to optimize performance. The PowerPC is compatible with the previous IBM POWER architecture. Thus, extensions to the reference PowerPC definition to address specific POWER features from previous architectures are included. However, this is expected to provide only a temporary bridge to existing applications, as subsequent PowerPC designs will follow their own plan.

The PowerPC features super-scalar architecture, which allows simultaneous dispatching of three instructions into the three independent execution units. These execution units are the integer, the floating point, and the branch processing unit. Simultaneous instructions can execute in parallel, and complete out of order, while the hardware ensures program correctness. The on-chip branch processing unit does hardware branch prediction, with reversal. Thirty two 32 bit registers are provided, and two modes of operation (supervisor and user) are implemented.

The PowerParallel systems based on SP-1 were limited to 64 units by the switch. An upgraded switch with faster speeds (4x) and lower latencies (6x) in SP-2 allows more than 128 processors to be usefully linked. (128 has been demonstrated.) The Switch is a bidirectional crossbar configuration, and uses an Intel i860 processor (section 5.4.5). A bidirectional transfer rate from application to application is 30 megabytes/second, with a latency less than 40 microseconds. The switch provides a communications path between processor modules, and an NFS connected file system. A shared-nothing approach is used. The switch provides an upper limit to connectivity, due to the complexity of expanding a crossbar switch.

Smaller systems do not need a switch, providing essentially a LAN/cluster in a box.

Two node types are defined, based on physical characteristics. The thin node has up to 512 Mbytes of memory, 4 Gbytes of disk, and 4 MCA slots. A wide node has up to 2 Gbytes of memory, 8 Gbytes of disk, and 7 MCA slots

Supported environments include Express, Linda, PVM, PVMe (optimized for the IBM switch), and AIXParallel. These systems support a series of debugging and profiling tools for the parallel environment.

Convex

Convex Computer has traditionally been known as a manufacturer of VAX compatible mini-supercomputers, known as the C series. Currently, the C3 and C4 models are available. However, their Exemplar machine uses the HP-Precision Architecture RISC approach with multiple HP workstation boxes in one cabinet, tied together with PVM software (parallel virtual machine, from Oak Ridge National Laboratory). These machines handle large amounts of on-line storage and fast I/O. They implement a loosely coupled parallel machine, and have software for load balancing and job allocation. Convex has a good view of what parallel processing technologies are acceptable and cost-effective in the marketplace. Depending on sales, the Vax compatible line may be dropped in favor of the massively parallel line. Convex machines make sense as an upper extension to existing

HP applications and workstations. Because of this, HP acquired Convex.

The Exemplar series run an implementation of HP's HP-UX, augmented by the OSF/1-Mach threaded microkernel, called SPP-UX. All of the HP-9000 series (section 5.3.9) software runs on the Exemplar in a binary compatible fashion. Also, Convex provides a version of the NQS software, for distributing jobs across multiple systems, and for load balancing. The Parallel Consultant toolkit provides for debug, test, and optimization of applications in the parallel environment.

The Exemplar supports up to 128 processors. These are organized as hypernodes of up to 8 processors connected by a crossbar, of bandwidth 2.5 gigabytes/second. Interconnect latency is on the order of 100's of nanoseconds. Each hypernode has its own memory which is shared among the processors in the hypernode. A hypernode can be thought of as a tightly coupled, shared memory SMP. I/O interfaces are distributed across the hypernodes, and support industry standards including SCSI, FDDI, and HIPPI.

A second level torroidal interconnect is used between hypernodes. This scale-able toroidal interconnect (sci) is based on the IEEE Scalable Coherent Interface (IEEE 1596-1992), and provides 4 unidirectional rings with a capacity of up to 2 gigabytes per second. Sequential access to memory are interleaved across the rings of the toroid, for load balancing. The hyper-node can be thought as a tightly coupled, fine-grained system, and the collection of hyper-nodes can be thought of as a coarse-grained, message-passing architecture. The overall machine has coherent distributed memory, and a large I/O system that is also distributed. Sixty four channels per I/O unit can be used, to a total of 4096 channels.

The Service processor functionality is distributed among the hypernodes, with options for boot, diagnostics, and monitoring. JTAG is used for diagnostic scans of the hardware. A systems console (service hypernode) is used, with a separate and independent DaRT (diagnostic and testing bus), that operates in parallel with the interconnect busses.

The Exemplar series from Convex best provides a seamless upper extenuation to the HP-9000 family. Software and applications can be migrated to a scalable and expandable environment. HP-UX hosted applications in c/c++ and Cobol can be migrated, implemented first as scalar code, and them parallelized as required, by the Convex toolset.

Tandem

Long known as a manufacturer of fault tolerant systems ("non-stop"), Tandem Computer took a corporate look at itself and decided it was really in the massively parallel business. The K100 series machines only provides 4 nodes and the K1000, with 16 nodes, are better suited to SMP. The K10000 can scale to over 4000 nodes. The Tandem machines used to use their own proprietary

CISC chip, but are now based on the MIPS R4400 RISC processor chip, and can be combined in a shared memory configuration.

Networking between nodes in the system takes one of several forms. For up to 16 cpu's, 4 gigabytes of memory, and 64 I/O channels, a Torus-Net internal networking architecture is used. For up to 224 cpu's, 57 gigabytes of memory, and 896 I/O channels, a variation called the TorusNet Domain is used. For the high end system, the multi-domain Torus-Net supports 4080 cpu's, 1 terabyte of main memory, and 16, 320 I/O channels. At each stage, disk resources scale with the cpu's. Besides up to 256 Megabytes of main memory per processor node, 4 megabytes of secondary cache are included. Each processor has 2 I/O channels. A K10000 multi-function controller node also uses dual MIPS processors, and supports 2 SCSI busses.

Each node of the machine runs the Tandem non-stop kernel, which is POSIX compliant. A single system image is maintained. A variety of 4GL's, CASE tools such as Texas Instruments' IEF, and the languages c, c++, and Cobol85 are supported. Oracle and Tandem's ANSI SQL database interfaces are available, as is the Tuxedo transaction monitor. The Non-Stop SQL/MP is an implementation of the SQL that takes specific advantage of the parallelism architecture of the Himalaya series. Queries are optimized according to a system 'cost' function, which takes into account system resources used. Parallel joins, scans, updates, deletes, inserts, and index builds are supported. A "Safeguard" security access facility provides for provisions against unauthorized access and modification of the data. Tandem wants to position itself as a leader in OLTP, and data warehousing. The 'Prism' warehouse manager system is used to migrate legacy data into a data warehouse on the system. Tandem has numerous commercial sales into this market for retail sales, telecommunications service providers, medical information firms, and manufacturers.

Unisys

Unisys, in conjunction with Novell and Intel, put together SPP (Scalable Parallel Processor) boxes with up to 128 Pentium class processors, linked with Intel's high speed interconnect technology at 175 Mbytes/second simultaneous I/O. Initial applications included Oracle's Parallel Query. The introduction of these systems was in early 1995. A shared I/O architecture is used, with I/O boards supporting SCSI and ethernet.

Unisys used Intel's iMRC chip-instantiation of the mesh interconnect to build MPP's. This wormhole routing interconnect scheme was originally developed for the Intel Paragon machines. It scales in units of 4x4. The Unisys machine ran Unix SVR4, and also Windows-NT. Unisys did the software, which made use of a microkernel, with a single system image. The product will be in testing 4Q94, with release scheduled for 2Q95. There was also a strategic alliance with Sequent.

Sun

Sun Microsystems, using SPARC technology, handles up to 20 PE units in an SMP arrangement. Sun Systems use the SPARC architecture and the Solaris operating system. SPARC chips are available from Texas Instruments and Fujitsu/Ross, as well as others. The Solaris operating system has become a popular choice for MPP developers as well.

The SPARCserver 1000 hosts up to 8 cpu's on the XDBbus. The high end SPARCcenter 2000 machine uses a packet switched backplane XDBbus, originally developed by XEROX. Essentially 2 buses in parallel, the interconnect achieves an aggregate 500 Mbytes/second. The architecture is shared memory, with up to 20 cpu's with 1 megabyte of local cache memory, and up to 20 banks of 256 megabyte RAM each. In addition, 10 S-buses of 4 slots each provide the I/O interface. Each S-bus can operate at 50 Mbytes/second. The S-bus interface is on the same board as the cpu. A S-bus can support SCSI, FDDI, and other popular interface standards. There is a central arbiter for the S-bus. JTAG is used for diagnostics.

SGI

Silicon Graphics, long known for its work in 3-D graphics, addressed the commercial markets in addition to its traditional engineering workstation niche. Although perceived as expensive options due to inherent graphics capabilities, the SGI systems were realigned to be price competitive with offering from other vendors. SGI has addressed the user concerns of mass storage and connectivity.

SGI computers use the MIPS chip architecture. SGI liked these so well they bought the company, acquiring and doubling the R&D budget for chip architectural design firm MIPS. The chips themselves are fabricated by various vendors such as IDT. MIPS, meaning Microprocessor without Interlocking Pipeline Stages, is a multi-sourced architecture, built to an Instruction set architecture (ISA) specification maintained by MIPS Computer Corp. The Challenge series uses the MIPS 4400 series chips, and the PowerChallenge series uses the R8000 chip.

The R8000 is a 64 bit, superscalar instantiation of the MIPS architecture, developed by MIPS Technologies, now owned by Silicon Graphics, and Toshiba. The emphasis of the R8000 is floating point intensive operations, where it achieves levels of performance comparable to a Cray Y-MP. The chip is also designed to support symmetric multiprocessing.

The R8000 project started in 1991, with a goal of bringing down the cost of supercomputing levels of performance to workstation levels. The approach was to gain an order of magnitude improvement in throughput from processor architecture and organization, and another order of magnitude from multiprocessing (SMP).

The R8000 can dispatch up to four instructions per clock

cycle. There are two floating point units, two load/store memory interface units, and two integer units. Out of order execution is supported for floating point, but not in the integer pipeline. It should be noted that floating point instructions are issued in order with respect to other floating point instructions in the stream, but may execute out-of-order with respect to integer instructions in the input stream. In essence, the floating and integer pipes are decoupled.

Initial silicon operates at 75 Mhz. With four issue, this translates to 300 mips. Two of the four can be double precision floating point. Simultaneously, two double precision loads or stores can be conducted. The integer ALU's and the shifter unit operate in one cycle. Double precision multiply can be accomplished in 6 cycles in the non-pipelined unit, and divide can take up to 73 cycles. The translation lookaside buffer is a dual ported, three way set associative cache of 384 entries. A random replacement algorithm is used.

The integer pipeline consists of 5 stages. ALU operations can occur in parallel with data cache access. A delay is incurred in the pipeline when an address from an ALU operation calculation is used as a base address for the following load or store. This is in contrast to the normal "load shadow" of a delayed load, whereby an instruction following a load cannot use the result of that load.

The floating point unit is implemented as an associated, tightly coupled R8010 chip. The architecture of the machine is 64 bit, with data structures and addressed being of this size. The R8000 is MIPS instruction set compatible, and implements a superset of the R4000 64 bit instruction set. New instructions include the fused multiply-add, register+register addressing for performance enhancement on arrays with arbitrary strides, and conditional moves on both integer and floating conditions. A 8 bit floating condition code set was added. Simple if-then-else constructs can compile to linear code.

Alignment-free instruction dispatching is provided by a queue that decouples the fetch pipeline from the dispatch logic. The chosen branch prediction schema matches the requirements for the object oriented programming paradigm, according to SGI.

The cache is split in an interesting way. Integer data references go to a 16 kbyte, dual ported, on-chip cache, but floating point references bypass this to an off-chip cache that can be up to 16 Mbytes. This external cache is two way interleaved, and four way set associative. The D-cache is virtually addressed, physically tagged. Coherency is enforced in hardware, and the D-cache is always a proper subset of the external cache. No write buffer is required, because the bandwidth of the external cache is such that it can accept full write-thru form the internal cache. The external cache is write-back.

An on-chip, 16 Kbyte directed mapped instruction cache is also used. It is refilled from external cache. The I-cache is virtually indexed and tagged. This is the result of extensive trades in favor of minimizing complexity from the instruction fetch path. On chip cache is filled from external cache over a 128 bit wide data path, in seven cycles for data, 11 cycles for instruction. A separate branch prediction cache of 1k entries is also provided.

The interconnect methodology of the SGI Challenge series is the E-bus backplane. This can support transfer rates to 1.2 Gigabits/second over a 256 bit wide data path. A shared memory and I/O architecture is used. The bus from one to nine processor subsystem boards, one to eight memory boards, and one to four I/O boards. The processor subsystem boards have dual processors with 1-4 megabytes of 4 way set associative unified streaming cache. The memory boards host 64 megabytes to 16 gigabytes of 2-way interleaved memory. The I/O boards host a series of industry standard interfaces, including vme-64, ethernet, fddi, hippi, atm, and scsi-II. The I/O boards support a bandwidth of up to 320 Megabytes per second per board.

The operating system software is IRIX, derived from Unix System V.4.2 as a 64 bit, SMP system. It is POSIX and X/Open compliant, as well as with the SVR4 ABI. C and c++ compilers and CASE tools are available.

As with all shared resource systems, particularly shared memory, the bus bandwidth becomes the bottleneck. Starting with a fast, wide backplane gives these systems a significant edge, but there is still an inherent upper limit to systems scalability into MPP class systems.

GigaMachine

Dressler Computer Technologie is a German company, that makes a GIGA-machine product from SPARC chips, and the Solaris operating system. They use the PVM software, and the Futurebus+ (64 bit wide). They only have two board types: one for compute and one for I/O. Configured with more I/O nodes than processor nodes, it becomes a file server. It supports 2 to 50 SPARC processors (contrast this with Meiko, TMC), 64 megabytes to 6 Gigabytes of memory, and in excess of a terabyte of disk, interfaced by fast and wide SCSI-II, in a RAID configuration. The calculation node, taking one backplane slot, has up to 4 processors with 1 megabyte of cache each, and 512 megabytes of memory. The I/O node uses two backplane slots, and provides 2 Mbus and 3 S-bus slots, as well as two processors with cache and RAM. They support Ethernet, token ring, FDDI, and ISDN, but there was no mention of HIPPI or ATM. The inherent limitation of the Futurebus for interprocessor communication will limit the scalability of this machine to just beyond current SMP levels.

BBN Butterfly

The Butterfly machine was built by Bolt, Baranek, and Newman in the 1980's.It had a butterfly-like multistage switching network for interprocessor communications. It could scale up to 512 cpu's with local memory. Each could access any of the other's memory, although at a cost in latency of roughly a factor of 15. The first Butterfly used Motorola 68000 processors. A 68101 was used later. The 3rd generation used the 68020's with memory management, The later models used the Motorola 88100 cpu's. The machine eventually ran the Mach kernel. The machine was numa, non-uniform memory access, and was a symmetric multiprocessor. Lawrence Livermore Laboratory got the largest configuration ever built.

GPU computing

The focus on large parallel machines has changed from clusters of general purpose ALU's to GPU's.

The graphics processing unit performs arithmetic operations on image data. These were introduced in the late 1990's as specialized architectures optimized for processing of large blocks of graphics data in parallel. Their instruction set is targeted to operations performed on 3D graphics data, such as transformations and rendering. Although these were originally targeted to computer gaming applications, it was not lost on scientists and engineers that this was the type of matrix manipulation and digital filtering that they employed in many different areas. The GPU is not general-purpose, but is targeted and optimized to operate on matrix data structures. GPU's are now used for many general-purpose scientific and engineering computing across a range of platforms. The term GPU was invented by high-performance graphics vendor nVidia.

Using high-level languages, GPU-accelerated applications can run the sequential part of the workload on a CPU, optimized for single-threaded performance, while running parallel processing on the GPU. This is called referred to as "GPU computing."

GPU computing is possible because today's GPU does a lot more than just render graphics: It might achieve a teraflop of floating point performance.

The first GPU's were designed as graphics accelerators, supporting only specific fixed-function pipelines. Starting in the late 1990s, the hardware became increasingly programmable. Less than a year after the GPU first appeared, it was being applied in various technical computing fields because of its excellent floating point performance. The General Purpose GPU, GPGPU as nVidia calls it, had appeared. Derived from that, we get GPU computing.

Initially, GPU's ran graphics programming languages such as OpenGL. Developers had to map scientific calculations onto problems that could be represented by triangles and polygons. A breakthrough came when a group of Stanford University researchers set out to re-purpose the GPU as a "streaming processor."

In 2003, *Brook* was introduced as the first widely adopted programming model to extend C with data-parallel constructs. Using concepts such as streams, kernels and reduction operators, the Brook compiler and runtime system presented the GPU as a general-purpose processor in a high-level language. Most importantly, Brook programs were not only easier to write than hand-tuned GPU code, they were many times faster. GPU's process high speed video data on phones, tablets, and tv's, and also find wide application in scientific and financial computing.

CUDA (Compute Unified Device Architecture) is a trademark of nVidia Corporation. It is a parallel computing platform and a programming model. It enables dramatic increases in computing performance by harnessing the power of the graphics processing unit (GPU). A CUDA program includes parallel functions (kernels) across parallel threads. The compiler organizes these threads into blocks and grids. A block is a set of concurrently executing threads that can synchronize and co-ordinate. A grid is an array of blocks. The CUDA programming model a thread has private memory. Each block has shared memory space, as do Grids.

Threads map to processors. Each Gpu unit executes one or more grids. Each streaming multiprocessor executes one or more thread blocks, and CUDA cores, and possibly other execution engines execute threads.

CUDA introduced a variation on the digital signal processing Multiply-Accumulate operation (AxB+C), called Fused Multiply-ADD (FMA). In traditional Multiply-Add the AxB product will be truncated, but in the FMA, all bits of the produce are retained for the ADD operation.

Applying the horsepower of the GPU to real problems, the CUDA allows applications to be written in c, c++,

Python and FORTRAN. NVIDIA unveiled CUDA in 2006 as a solution for general-computing on GPU's.

The G-80 chip, introduced in 2006, established the GPU computing model. It supported the c programming language, and was threaded. It implemented the Single Instruction, Multiple thread concept. It had a complexity of 680 million-1.4 billion transistors. It did not include L1 or L2 cache.
Fermi.

The Fermi architecture was released in 2010, as a significant improvement over the G-80. It implemented up to 512 CUDA cores, each executing an integer or floating point operation pr clock. CUDA cores, and required 3 billion transistors. The chip supported c++, OpenCL, and DirectCompute. It featured full IEEE floating point, single and double precision. It implemented on chip L1 and L2 caches. The GigaThread™ engine allowed for concurrent kernel execution, and out-of-order thread block execution. Both L1 and L2 cache were included. The architecture was 32-bit. A new instruction set architecture (ISA) supported parallel thread execution via a virtual machine.

Kepler

The Kepler GK110 CUDA chip is constructed from over 7 billion transistors, and provides a TeraFlop (10^{12}) of double-precision floating point operations per second. This is a performance increase of a factor of three over its predecessor, the Fermi model. The high-end model

149

includes dynamic parallelism, which adjusts and controls the scheduling in the GU without the intervention of the CPU. GPU utilization is enhanced by a technique known as Hyper-Q, which allows multiple cpu cores to use a single GPU, up to 32.

The unit can include up to 15 SMX processor units, and six 64-bit memory controllers. There is a 1536 kbytes of L2 Cache on chip. SMX is nVidia's term for the Streaming Microprocessor architecture. SMX has 8 instruction dispatch engines, a 32-bit register files of size 65,536, 64 kbytes of shared memory/L1 cache, and a 48k read-only data cache. This cache is reserved for data values known (by the compiler) not to change, and thus no cache writes are required. It also includes 192 CUDA cores, 64 double-precision arithmetic units, 32 special function units (SFU), and 32 load/store units. The CUDA cores include both integer and floating point capability,. The special function units assist in transcendental computations.

A group of 32 threads than can operate in parallel is called a warp. Up to 4 warps can be executing simultaneously. Thread scheduling is done in hardware, but based on information from the compiler ("hints') concerning dependencies and data hazards. The compiler is a critical part of scheduling threads for best efficiency. The threads are allocated up to 255 per thread. A special instruction allows executing threads to share data without going through shared memory. Atomic memory operations are provided to ensure consistency among threads.

Texture filtering units (TFU's) are provided in the architecture, with each SMS having 16.

All on-chip memory is single-error-correct, double-error-detect. If a cache line is found to be invalid, a new read operation is automatically generated. Fetches from external DRAM are protected by an error-correcting code.

Design & Construction of Loyola's 64 Node Parallel Processor

This section describes the design & construction of a 64 node parallel processor based on the Inmos Transputer, for the graduate engineering program at Loyola College, now Loyola University Maryland. This project provided valuable hands-one experience to staff and students, and resulted in a valuable institutional resource for other programs, such as for the development of software courses.

In June 1992, Loyola had most of the parts needed to integrate a 64 node parallel processor at the Columbia lab, thanks to generous donations from Inmos Corp. We had on hand sufficient T414 Transputer processors, over 500 pieces of SRAM memory, multiple copies of the development software system, and numerous technical reports and data books.

At the lab in Columbia, we had set up a Transputer development workstation, hosted in a PC, that allowed us to develop code for the parallel machine in 'c', Pascal, FOR-TRAN, or Occam. This system, consisting of a single Transputer at present, is used for student projects. Later, we duplicated this development system.

Besides the experience gained by building and demonstrating this unit, other departments at Loyola were seen to benefit. Engineering Science was providing a resource that others could use. For example, ongoing projects at Loyola included using parallel processing for image processing research, using Transputers for embedded robot control, and setting up a parallel processing course.

Out target was to do this project at a minimum cost, using existing and donated resources, and student labor. Engineering Science would then provide the use of the machine as a resource to students in our program, and for other departments. The parts budget was $4000.

A 4-node Transputer board was prototyped and designed by a Loyola alumnus. The 4 node board was designed to be used as 4, 1 node boards, or a single 4 node configuration. We originally planned to procure several Augat-style wire-wrap boards. Each node of the parallel processor machine will require a Transputer chip, a clock source, memory, and several "glue" chips. A design for the node was completed. A node was estimated to take 3 hours to wire-wrap, and 2 hours to checkout and debug. Each Augat card could hold 8-10 nodes. However, experience with wire-wrapped Transputer systems showed significant electrical noise and interference problems with the memory interface. The circuit board approach was chosen. Sixteen of the boards, plus two spares were produced, to house the donated Transputers.

Similarly, we originally planned to make use of the donated SRAM for the system memory. Each node was to have, at a minimum, 256k bytes of memory, for a total of 16 Megabytes system memory. We did not have, however, enough of pin-compatible memory to use for the 16 boards, without doing several derivative designs. Thus, we switched to purchased SRAM chips for the design. The SRAM chips were the most expensive procured component of the system. In a Transputer system, the memory must be 32 bits wide, forcing use of 4 pieces of byte wide memory.

The quad board was able to use a single 5 MHz clock oscillator for all four nodes on the board. Transputers' links were connected to nearest neighbor, and the spare links were buffered off board using TTL drivers. Inmos standard up, down, and system control system resources were provided. A quad board drew 100mA at 5 volts, for 4 Transputers with 256k of external memory each.

The boards were assembled, populated, and checked out over the summer of 1993 by students. All of the boards and chips worked as planned. After unit test, an integrated system was built up as interconnect cables were fabricated.

The system was completed in November of 1993 with the design and construction of a power distribution board. Checkout was particularly easy, using the most rudimentary of software tools. The complexity of the system was much less than that of an integer processor of the same parts count, because in the case of the parallel processor, it was 64 identical, replicated circuits. Using only the Public domain software utilities CHECK and MTEST, we were able to debug the hardware in one evening. The software was tell us the node that had an error, which mapped to a particular board. For memory problems, we had the node and the byte, which mapped to a chip. In most cases a cursory visual inspection would reveal a missed solder joint, or an incorrect chip.

As of 1994, a card cage was being fabricated for the machine, to protect the board interconnect cables. Plans were being made to connect the parallel processor's host machine, a 80386, to the network, and thence to the Internet. A graduate level course on parallel programmed was proposed, based on the machine. And, faculty members were exploring the feasibility of using the machine for code previously run on a Cray. Studies of the SPRINT-2 architecture, a similar system using 64 Transputers, showed it to have an equivalent speed of execution to that of a Cray Y-MP.

Beowulf

(The following is abstracted from the Wikipedia article.

Originally referring to a specific computer built in 1994, *Beowulf* now refers to a class of computer clusters similar to the original system developed at NASA's Goddard Space Flight Center. Originally developed by Thomas Sterling and Donald Becker. Beowulf systems are now

154

deployed worldwide, chiefly in support of scientific computing. They are high-performance parallel computing clusters of inexpensive pc hardware. The name comes from the main character in the Old English poem Beowulf which was bestowed by Sterling because the describes the Beowulf as having "thirty men's heft of grasp in the gripe of his hand."

A Beowulf cluster is a group of what are normally identical, commercially available computers, which are running a Free & Open Source Software (FOSS), Unix-like operating system, such as bsd, gnu/Linux, or Solaris. They are networked into a small tcp/ip lan and have libraries and programs installed which allow processing to be shared among them.

There is no_particular piece of software that defines a cluster as a Beowulf. Commonly used parallel processing libraries include Message Passing Interface (MPI) and Parallel virtual Machine (PVM). Both of these permit the programmer to divide a task among a group of networked computers, and collect the results of processing. Examples of MPI software include OpenMPI or MPICH. There are additional MPI implementations available.

Provisioning of Operating System and other software for a Beowulf Cluster can be automated using available software, packages, such as Open Source Cluster Application Resources (OSCAR) OSCAR installs on top of a standard installation of a supported GNU/Linux distribution on a cluster's head node.

A simple Beowulf cluster can be constructed with surplus pc's on wooden shelves, or can be a rack of high performance servers. Several company's offer commercial clusters.

The following is the definition of a Beowulf cluster from the original *how-to* which was published by Jacek Radajewski and Douglas Eadline under the Linux Documentation Project in 1998:

Beowulf is a multi-computer architecture which can be used for parallel computations It is a system which usually consists of one server node, and one or more client nodes connected together via Ethernet or some other network. It is a system built using commodity hardware components, like any PC capable of running a Unix-like operating system, with standard Ethernet adapters, and switches. It does not contain any custom hardware components and is trivially reproducible. Beowulf also uses__commodity software like the GNU/Linux or Solaris operating system, Parallel Virtual Machine (PVM) and Message Passing Interface (MPI)The server node controls the whole cluster and serves files to the client nodes. It is also the cluster's console and gateway to the outside world. Large Beowulf machines might have more than one server node, and possibly other nodes dedicated to particular tasks, for example consoles or monitoring stations. In most cases client nodes in a Beowulf system are dumb, the dumber the better. Nodes are configured and controlled by the server node, and do only what they are told to do. In a disk-less client configuration, a client node doesn't even know its IP address or name until the server tells it.

One of the main differences between Beowulf and a Cluster of Workstations (COW) is that Beowulf behaves more like a single machine rather than many workstations. In most cases client nodes do not have keyboards or monitors, and are accessed only via remote login or possibly serial terminal. Beowulf nodes can be thought of as a CPU + memory package which can be plugged in to the cluster, just like a CPU or memory module can be plugged into a motherboard.

Beowulf is not a special software package, new network topology, or the latest kernel hack. Beowulf is a technology of clustering computers to form a parallel, virtual supercomputer. Although there are many software packages such as kernel modifications, PVM and MPI libraries, and configuration tools which make the Beowulf architecture faster, easier to configure, and much more usable, one can build a Beowulf class machine using standard GNU/Linux distribution without any additional software. If you have two networked computers which share at least the /home file system via NFS, and trust each other to execute remote shells (rsh), then it could be argued that you have a simple, two node Beowulf machine.

A cluster can be set up by using the Knoppix bootable CDs in combination with OpenMosix. The computers will automatically link together, without need for complex configurations, to form a Beowulf cluster using all

CPUs and RAM in the cluster. A Beowulf cluster is scalable to a nearly unlimited number of computers, limited only by the overhead of the network.

The very latest in Beowulf clusters is one based on the Raspberry Pi computer, which is based on the 32-bit ARM processor. The board is the size of a deck of cards.

Glossary of Terms

3GL   third generation (computer) language, COBOL, Fortran, c

4GL   fourth generation (computer) language, non-procedural

5GL   fifth generation (computer) language - usually object oriented

68k   CISC architecture from Motorola

80x86   CISC family from Intel, 8086, 80286, 80287, 80386, 80486, etc.

88k   RISC architecture from Motorola

ABI   applications binary interface

acronym   a resident of Akron, Ohio

Ada   standard computer language, required for DoD projects

AI   artificial intelligence

AIX   Advanced Interactive Executive, IBM's Unix

alc   assembly language code

ALLCACHE   trademark memory architecture from KSR

Alpha   64 bit RISC architecture from Digital Equipment Corp.

alu   arithmetic logic unit

ansi   American National Standards Institute

API   Application Programming Interface

ARPA   Advanced Research Projects Agency

ASCII   American Standard Code for Information Interchange, a 7 bit code

async   asynchronous

ATM   Asynchronous Transfer Mode - a WAN
      technology
AViiON   computer system from Data General
asic   application specific integrated circuit
B1   a level of computer systems security defined
      by DoD
baud   rate of information transfer, in
            symbols/second
bear   bus error address register (Intel i860)
Bellcore   Bell Communications Research
BER   bit error rate
BiCMOS   technology blend of bipolar and CMOS
big-endian having the least significant byte in a word on
            the right
B-ISDN   binary integrated services digital network
bit   the smallest unit of binary information
BLOB   Binary Large Object, usually applied
            to image data
Booth   Algorithm for fast binary multiplication
bpi   bits per inch
bsd   Berkeley Systems Distribution (Unix)
bus   a parallel data pathway
byte   a collection of 8 bits
c   computer language developed at Bell Labs
in 1972
C2   DoD security level for systems, providing
            controlled access
c++   object oriented computer language
cache   a small, fast memory between the processor
            and the main memory
CalTech   California Institute of Technology

can	campus area network
case	computer aided software environment (tools)
CCITT	French acronym, "Comite Consultaif Internationale de Telegraphique et Telephonique"
CD-ROM	Compact disk, read-only memory channel point-point connection between two processes
CHMOS	variation on CMOS
CISC	complex instruction set computer
CM*	early research multiprocessor at CMU
C.MMP	early research multiprocessor at CMU
CMOS	complementary metal-oxide semiconductor
CMU	Carnegie-Mellon University
COBOL	computer language, ANSI X3.23-1985
cold	computer output to laserdisk
comm	communications
cpu	central processor unit
CSMA/CD	LAN access technique - carrier sense multiple access/ collision detection
CWP	current word pointer; current window pointer
DARPA	Defense Advanced Research Projects Agency
DASD	direct access storage device
datacomm	data communications
DB-2	database software from IBM
DBMS	Database management system
D-cache	data cache
DCE	distributed computing environment - OSF approach to interconnectivity

DEC	Digital Equipment Corporation
demux	demultiplex
DG	Data General Corp.
dma	direct memory addressing - I/O to/from memory without processor involvement
DoD	(U.S.) Department of Defense
DOE	Department of Energy
DOS	Disk operating system
dram	dynamic random access memory
dsp	digital signal processing
D-tlb	data-TLB, see 'TLB'
ecl	emitter coupled logic, a common mode logic
that is	fast and uses power
ecc	error correcting code
EIA	Electronic Industries Association
eisa	extended industry standard bus (32 bit) (see ISA)
EL-90	Supercomputer from Cray Research, Inc.
E-mail	electronic mail
EMI	electromagnetic interference
ESDI	enhanced small device interface
Ethernet	a bit serial LAN communication protocol,
usually	10 mbps over coax cable
exa	prefix, 10^{18}
fddi	fibre distributed data interface
FIBRE Channel	emerging standard for data transmission
FIPS	Federal Information Processing Standards
Floating Point	a scientific/engineering representation scheme with a mantissa and an exponent
FUD	fear, uncertainty, doubt
Futurebus	a 32/64 bit backplane bus

GIPS	Giga (10^9) Operations per second
GFLOPS	Giga (10^9) Floating Point Operations per second
GOSIP	Government Open Systems Interconnection Profile
GPU	Graphics Processing Unit
GUI	graphical user interface
Harvard	computer architecture characterized by separate instruction and data paths
hippi	high performance parallel interface, an ansi standard
HP	Hewlett-Packard Co.
HP-PA	HP's Precision Architecture chip
HP-UX	HP's Unix
hypercube	topology in which each node is the vertex of an Order-n cube
HyperSPARC	SPARC implementation from Ross Technologies
Hz	Hertz, cycles per second
IBM	International Business Machines
I-cache	instruction cache
IEEE	Institute of Electronic and Electronic Engineers
IEF	Information Engineering Facility
IGES	Initial Graphics Exchange Standard
hot swap	to exchange modules without powering down
i860 addresses	high performance RISC chip from Intel, floating point performance
i960	RISC chip from Intel, addressed embedded and military markets

ic	integrated circuit
IDT	company name - Integrated Device Technology
iMRC	Intel's mesh router component (chip)
Intel SSD	Intel Supercomputer Systems Division
I/O	Input/Output
ipd	interactive parallel debugger
IPI	intelligent peripheral interface
iPSC	computer line from Intel Corp.
ISA	industry standard architecture (16 bit bus); instruction set architecture
isdn	integrated services digital network
ISO	International Standards Organization
I-tlb	instruction TLB, see 'TLB'
iWarp	a processor architecture from Intel Corp.
JPEG	Joint Photographic Experts Group
jtag	(IEEE) Joint Test Action Group
jukebox	automated handler for storage media
k	(prefix) 1024
Kerboros	communications security algorithm from MIT
kernel	a process providing basic services
KSR	Kendall Square Research, MPP vendor
LAN	local area network
Linpack	a benchmark for scientific applications
LIPS	Logical inferences per second
LISP	AI language, list-processing, derived from McCarthy at MIT
little-endian	having the least significant byte of a word on the right
LOC	Library of Congress, roughly, 10 terabytes

	of text
longword	usually, a 64 bit word
LRU	least recently used (replacement algorithm)
lsb	least significant bit, or byte
Mach	multitasking Unix kernal from CMU
man	Metropolitan Area Network
Mbus	memory bus architecture from Sun Microsystems
MCA	micro channel architecture (32 bit bus)
MCA-E	micro channel architecture - extended (64 bit)
mesh	topology in which nodes form a regular acyclic n-dimensional grid
MESI	Modified, Exclusive, Shared, Invalid cache protocol for multiprocessing
MFLOPS	Mega (10^6) Floating Point Operations per second
Mhz	megahertz
micron	10^-6 meter
MIMD	multiple instruction, multiple data computer architecture model
MIPS	Mega (10^6) Operations per second; also, a company name
MISD	multiple instruction, single data computer architecture model
MIT	Massachusetts Institute of Technology
MMU	memory management unit
MOS	metal oxide semiconductor
Motif	GUI from OSF for X-Windows
mpp	massively parallel processor
MPU	main processor unit

msb	most significant bit, or byte
MTTF	mean time to failure
MTTR	mean time to repair
Mux	multiplex
NaN	not-a-number (bit pattern used for status in floating point)
nand	logic function, negated 'and'
NASA	National Aeronautics and Space Administration
NCR	computer manufacturer, ex-National Cash Register
NCSC	National Computer Security Center
nCube	a computer company, and a computer
NEC	Nippon Electric Corporation, manufacturer
of chips	and computers
nfs	network file system
NIST	National Institute of Standards & Technology, (nee, National Bureau of Standards)
NMI	non-maskable interrupt
nor	logic function, negated 'or'
NQS	network queuing system - batch software for networks
nxor	logic function, negated XOR
oem	Original Equipment Manufacturer
OLCP	On-line complex processing
OLE	object linking and embedding
OLTP	On line transaction processing
OO	object oriented
OODBMS	object oriented database management system
OOPS	object oriented programming system

opcode	operation code; instruction
opsys	operating system
OS	operating system
OSF	Open Software Foundation
OSF-1	Open Software Foundation OS, based on Mach
OSI	Open Systems Interconnection
packet	a block of information
PAD	packet assembler/disassembler
PALcode	in DEC Alpha architecture, extends instruction set
palmtop	a small computer
PARC	Palo Alto Research Center, Xerox Corp.
pc	personal computer
PCI	peripheral component interconnect
pcmcia	Personal Computer Memory Card Industry Association
Pcode	pseudocode
PDN	public data network
Pentium 80x86	Intel processor, instruction set compatible to family; would be 80586
Peta	prefix, 10^{15}
PE	processor element, usually consisting of cpu, memory, I/O
pga	pin grid array (package of integrated circuits)
Pipeline	an assembly line type processing of instruction execution
pixel	picture element
pmmu	paged memory management unit
POSIX	Portable Operating System Interface for

Unix -	IEEE standard
PostScript	a page description language by Adobe Sytems
PowerPC	RISC chip by Motorola, IBM, Apple Computer
PQFP	plastic quad flat pack (for integrated circuit)
PRDBMS	parallel relational data base management system
PRISM	parallel reduced instruction set multiprocessor - Apollo Computer
pse	parallel software environment
PSR	processor status (state) register
PVM domain	(software) parallel virtual machine, a public package from Oak Ridge National Laboratory, Dept. of Energy
quadword	4 words
R2000	32 bit early MIPS risc processor
R3000	32 bit MIPS risc processor
R4000	64 bit MIPS risc processor
R8000	64 bit MIPS processor, with speed of Cray Y-MP
RAID	Redundant Array of Inexpensive Disks
ram	random access memory
RDBMS	relational data base management system
ring	topology in which each node is connected to two others in a closed loop
RIOS	IBM RISC architecture; a chipset
RISC	reduced instruction set computer
RS-232-c	EIA specification for serial interconnect
RS/6000	IBM workstation
S-bus	I/O bus from Sun Microsystem

sci	Scalable component interconnect, IEEE 1596-1992 standard
SCO	Santa Cruz Operation, variant of Unix
SCSI	small computer system interface
SFU	special function unit (in Motorola architecture)
SGI	Silicon Graphics, Incorporated, computer manufacturer
SISD	single instruction, single data computer architecture model
SIMD	single instruction, multiple data computer architecture model
Smalltalk	object oriented computer language
smp	symmetric multi processor, or processing
SONET	synchronous optical network standard
SNA	systems network architecture
SP-1, SP-2	IBM RISC systems
SPARC	Scalable Processor ARChitecture
SPEC	System Performance Evaluation Cooperative, vendor association
SQL	structured query language
sram	static random access memory
stack	a first in, last out data structure
Sun	Sun Microsystems, computer manufacturer
SuperSPARC	SPARC chip from Texas Instruments
SVR4	(unix) system 5 (V), release 4
sync	synchronous; synchronized
T1	digital carrier at 1.544 Mbps
T3D	MPP machine from Cray Research, Inc.
TCP/IP	transmission control protocol / internet protocol

TI	Texas Instruments, computer and chip manufacturer
TIFF	Tag Image File Format - image exchange standard
TIPS	Tera (10^{12}) operations per second
TFLOPS	Tera (10^{12})Floating Point operations per second
TLB	translation lookaside buffer, used for virtual to physical memory mapping
TMC	Thinking Machines Corp.
torus	topology in which nodes from a regular cyclic n-dimensional grid
TPC	transaction processing council
tps	transactions per second
Transputer	a computer architecture from Inmos, Inc. tree acyclic graph; usually refers to a binary tree, where a node has two children, or branches
ttl	transistor-transistor logic
Ultrix	DEC Unix
Unicos	Unix variation from Cray Research, Inc.
unified cache	a cache memory that holds both instructions and data
Unix	operating system
USL	Unix Systems Lab
VAX	Virtual Architecture Extended - 32 bit minicomputer from DEC
VMS	operating system for VAX computers
word	a collection of bits; may be 4, 8, 16,18, 32, 64, 24, etc.
VESA	(bus) video electronics standards association

VLIW   very long instruction word
VLSI   Very Large Scale Integration; also, a
            company name
VME   (bus) versa bus extended
VME-64   Rev. D of the vme bus specification; 64 bits
Von Neumann computer architecture, control flow, data
and   instructions share memory
VUP   Vax unit of performance, roughly, 1 mip
wan   Wide Area Network
WIMP   Window, Icon, Menu, Pointer
Windows   operating system with GUI, from Microsoft
            Corp.
Windows-NT Windows-New Technology Operating
            System
WORM   Write once, read many (or, mostly)
XDBbus   high speed interconnect developed by Sun
            and XEROX-PARC
X-MP   supercomputer from Cray Research
xor   logic function, exclusive 'or'; either but not
            both
X-windows GUI, under Unix
X/Open   consortium for CAE
Y-MP   supercomputer from Cray Research, follows
            X-MP

General Bibliography

Abnous, Arthur and Bagherzadeh, Nader. "Architectural Design And Analysis Of A VLIW Processor," Computers & Electrical Engineering v 21 n 2 Mar 1995. p 119-142 1995 ISSN: 0045-7906.

Admiraal, J.C. and Carmichael, N. "Memory Managers for Transputer Networks," Applying Transputer Based Parallel Machines, 1989, IOS, ISBN 90-5199-011-1.

Agrawal, Rakesh, and Bell, David. "Databases in Parallel and Distributed Systems," 1990, IEEE Comp. Society Press.

Amdahl, G.M. "Validity of the Single Processor Approach to Achieving Large Scale Computing Capabilities," April, 1967, AFIPS Conference Proceedings.

Ashton, Gary A. (et al). "NML Storage Technology Assessment Final Report," July 1994, National Media Lab.

Austin, Murray, P. and Wellings, K. "The Design of an Operating System for a Scalable Parallel Computing Engine," Software, Practise & Experience, Oct 01 1991 v 21 n 10 p 989.

Bagrodia, Rajive L. "High Level Parallel Programming,"

August 1992, UCLA Computer Science Dept., RL-TR-92-215.

Bell, C. Gordon, Mudge, J. Craig, McNamara, John E. Computer Engineering A DEC view of Hardware System Design, Digital Press, 1978, ISBN 0932376002.

Board, John A. Jr. (ed). Transputer Research and Applications 2, 1990, IOS, ISBN 90 5199 027 .

Bode, Arndt (ed);Dal Cin, Mario (ed) P*arallel Computer Architectures : Theory, Hardware, Software, Applications*. Berlin; New York : Springer-Verlag, 1993, ISBN-0387573070.

Boman, Erik. "Experiences on the KSR1 Computer," Report RNP-93-008, April, 1993, NASA/Ames Research Center.

Borkar, S., Cohn, R., Cox, G. "Supporting Systolic and Memory Communication in iWarp," Computer Architecture News, 1990 v 18 n 2 Page: 70.

Braner, Moshe. "Brenda --- A Tool for Parallel Programming," 1985, Cornell Theory Center.

Braunl, Thomas *Parallel Computing: An Introduction* Park Ridge, N.J.: Noyes Data Corp., 1993, ISBN-0133368270.

Brehm, Jurgen. *Parallele lineare Algebra: parallele*

Losungen ausgewahlter linearer Gleichungssysteme bei unterschiedlichen Multiprozessor-Architekturen Wiesbaden: Deutscher UniversitatsVerlag, 1992.

Breit, Stephen R. Pangali, Cahni, Zirl, David M. "Technical Applications on the KSR1: High Performance and Ease of Use," P. IEEE Compcon'93, San Francisco, Ca., Feb. 1993 pps. 303-310.

Burke, Edmund. "An Overview of System Software for the KSR1," P. IEEE Compcon'93, San Francisco, Ca. Feb. 1993 pps. 295-299.

Capon, Peter C. "Experiments in Algorithmic Parallelism," Applying Transputer Based Parallel Machines, 1989, IOS, ISBN 90-5199-011-1.

Capon, Peter C. "Experiments in Algorithmic Parallelism," Applying Transputer Based Parallel Machines, 1989, IOS, ISBN 90-5199-011-1.

Carriero, Nicholas and Gelernter, David. "Linda in Context," Communications of the ACM, APR 01 1989 v 32 n 4 P 444.

Casavant, Thomas L. (Author, Ed); Tvrdik, Pavel(Ed); Plasil, Frantisek (Ed) *Parallel Computers: Theory And Practice,* Los Alamitos, Calif.: IEEE Computer Society Press, 1995, ISBN 0818651628.

Chen, Peter M., et al. "RAID: High Performance,

Reliable Secondary Storage," Oct. 1993, ACM Computing Surveys.

Cheriton, David R., Goosen, Hendrick A., and Boyle, Patrick D. "Paradigm: A Highly Scalable Shared-Memory Multicomputer Architecture," Computer, Feb 01 1991 v 24 n 2 p 33.

Cole, Bernard C. "Scaling the Limits," Electronic Engineering Times. Feb. 15, 1993.

Collier, William W. Reasoning About Parallel Architectures Englewood Cliffs, N.J.: Prentice Hall, 1992.

Crichlow, Joel M. *An Introduction to Distributed and Parallel Computing*, 1988, Prentice-Hall, ISBN 0-13-481086-4.

Davy, John R. (ed); Dew, Pater M. (ed) *Abstract Machine Models For Highly Parallel Computers* Oxford; New York: Oxford University Press, 1995, ISBN-0198537964.

DeCegama, Angel L. *Parallel Processing Architectures And VLSI Hardware* Englewood Cliffs, N.J.: Prentice-Hall, 1989, ASIN: B000OIXKLO.

DeGroot, A.J., Johansson, E.M., Fitch, J.P., Grant, C.W., Parker, S.R. "SPRINT - The Systolic Processor with a Reconfigurable Interconnection Network of

Transputers," IEEE T. Nuclear Science, Vol. NS-34, No. 4, August 1987, pp. 873-877.

del Rosario, Juan Miguel, Choundary, Alok N. "High-Performance I/O for Massively Parallel Computers. Problems and Prospects," March 1994, IEEE Computer.

Desrochers, George R. *Principles of Parallel and Multiprocessing*, 1987, Intertext, McGraw-Hill, ISBN 0-07-016579-3.

Dongarra, J. J. (ed). "Experimental Parallel Computer Architecture," 1987, Elsevier, ISBN 0-444-70234-2.

Ferscha, Alois. Modellierung Und Leistungsanalyse Paralleler Systeme Mit Dem PRM-Netz-Modell Wien: Oldenbourg, 1995.

Figueiredo, Marco. "An Architectural Comparison between the Inmos Transputer T800 and the Intel iWARP Microprocessors," 1990, Loyola College, Dept. of Engineering Science.

Fijany, A. and Bejczy, A. "Parallel Architecture for Robotics Computation,". NASA/JPL, NASA Tech Brief Vol. 14, No. 6, JPL invention Report NPO-17629/7126.

Fijany, A.; Bejczy, A. *Algorithmically Specialized Parallel Architecture for Robotics*,NASA/JPL, NASA Tech Brief Vol. 15, No. 2, JPL invention Report NPO-17632/7130.

Fijany, A.; Bejczy, A. *Parallel Architecture for Robotics Computation*, NASA/JPL, NASA Tech Brief Vol. 14, No. 6, JPL invention Report NPO-17629/7126.

Fillo, Marco, 1963- Architectural Support For Scientific Applications On Multicomputers 1. Aufl. Konstanz: Hartung-Gorre Verlag, 1993.

Fisher, Joseph A. "VLIW Machine: A Multiprocessor For Compiling Scientific Code," Computer v 17 n 7 Jul 1984 p 45-52 1984 ISSN: 0018-9162.

Fisher, Joseph. "Very Long Instruction Work Architecture And The Eli-512,"Annual Symposium on Computer Architecture 10th. IEEE, New York, NY,1983.

Fisher, Joseph A., Landskov, David, Shriver, Bruce D. "Microcode Compaction: Looking Backward And Looking Forward," AFIPS Conference Proceedings - 1981 National Computer Conference. Conference Chicago, Ill, 1981 May 4-7 AFIPS Conference Proceedings v 50, 1981. Publ by AFIPS Press, Arlington, VA., p 95-102 1981 ISSN: 0095-6880.

Fisher, Joseph A. "Microprogramming, Microprocessing And Supercomputing," Supercomputers: Technology and Applications: Fourteenth EUROMICRO Symposium on Microprocessing - EUROMICRO '88 Zurich, Switz: 1988 Aug 29-Sep 1 Microprocessing and Microprogramming v 24 n 1-5 Aug 1988. p 17-20 1988.

Fisher, Joseph A. "New Architecture For Supercomputing," Digest of Papers - COMPCON Spring 87: Thirty-Second IEEE Computer Society International Conference. San Francisco, CA, 1987 Feb 23-27 IEEE, New York, NY, Cat n 87CH2409-1, Piscataway, NJ, USA p 177-180, 1987.

Fisher, Joseph A. and Freudenberger, Stefan M. "Predicting Conditional Branch Directions From Previous Runs Of A Program," Proceedings of the 5th International Conference on Architectural Support for Programming Languages and Operating Systems: Boston, MA, E. I. International Conference on Architectural Support for Programming Languages and Operating Systems - ASPLOS 1992. ACM, New York, NY, p 85-95 1992.

Fisher, Joseph A. "Trace Scheduling: A Technique For Global Microcode Compaction," IEEE Transactions on Computers v C-30 n 7 Jul 1981 p 478-490: ISSN: 0018-9340.

Fisher, Joseph A. "2**N-Way Jump Microinstruction Hardware And An Effective Instruction Binding Method," MICRO 13, Annual Microprogram Workshop, 13th, Colorado Springs, CO, Nov 30-Dec 3 1980. IEEE Cat n 80CH1599-0, Piscataway, NJ, 1980, ISSN: 0361-2163.

Flynn, M. J. "Some Computer Organizations and their Effectiveness," Sept. 72, IEEE T. Computer, C-21, No. 9, pp. 948-960.

Forrest, B. M., Roweth, D. Stroud, N. Wallace D. J.Wilson, G. V. "Implementing Neural Network Models on Parallel Computers," 1987, The Computer Journal, Vol. 30, No. 5.

Freeman, T. L.; Phillips, C. *Parallel Numerical Algorithms* New York: Prentice Hall, 1992, ISBN-0136515975.

Garcia, Russ. "Future Directions In Disk-Drive Electronics," April 1995, Computer Design, p. 137.

Geist, Al, et al, *PVM--Parallel Virtual Machine: A Users' Guide And Tutorial For Networked Parallel Comput*ing Cambridge, Mass.: MIT Press, 1994, ISBN-0262571080.

Gelernter, David. "Getting the Job Done: The Linda Language Can Help Parallelize Existing Software And Develop New Program Structures," Byte, Nov. 1988 v 13 n 12 p 301.

George, Alan D. and Lois Wright Hawkes. "Microprocessor-Based Parallel Architecture for Reliable Digital Signal Processing". 1992, ISBN 0-8493-7176-7.

Ghosh, J.; Harrison C. (ed). "Parallel Architecture for Image Processing,," 1990, SPIE Proceedings, Vol. 1246.

179

Ghosh, Joydeep (ed); Harrison, C. G.; Watson, Thomas J. *Parallel Architecture for Image Processing,* SPIE Proceedings, Vol. 1246, 1990, ASIN 0819402931.

Gibbons, Alan (ed); Spirakis, Paul (ed)*Lectures On Parallel Computation* Cambridge; New York: Cambridge University Press, 1993; paperback edition, 2005, ISBN – 0521017602.

Gropp, William et al *Using MPI: Portable Parallel Programming With The Message-Passing Interface* 2nd ed, MIT Press, 1994, ISBN-0262571323.

Gross, T., Hinrichs, S., Lueh, G. "Compiling Task and Data Parallel Programs for iWarp," ACM SIGPLAN notices, 1993 v 28 n 1 Page: 32

Habiger, Claus. An Investigation Into The Cost-Effectiveness Of Multi-Chip Modules For Massively Parallel Computing Applications 1. Aufl. Konstanz: Hartung-Gorre, 1995.

Hammond, Kevin. Parallel SML: A Functional Language And Its Implementation In Dactl London: Pitman, 1991.

Harrison, M. A. (et al). *Advanced Computing in Japan,* Oct. 1990, published by the Japanese Technology Evaluation Center of Loyola College in Maryland, NTIS Report PB90-215765.

Hayes, Brian. "Computer with its Head Cut Off,"

American Scientist v 83 n 2 Mar-Apr 1995. p 126-130 1995 ISSN: 0003-0996.

Jacklin, Stephan A. et al. "High-Speed, Automatic Controller Design Consideration for Integrating Array Processor, Multi-Microprocessor, and Host Computer System Architecture," NASA/Ames Research Center, Tech Brief ARC-11670, Vol. 11, No. 3.

Heidrich, Dietmar; Grossetie, J. C. *Computing With T.Node Parallel Architecture* Dordrecht; Boston: Kluwer Academic Publishers, 1991, ISBN 9401055467.

Hockney, Roger W.; Jesshope, C. R. *Parallel Computers: Architecture, Programming, And Algorithms* 2nd ed. Bristol, England; Philadelphia, PA, USA: A. Hilger, 1988, ISBN 0852748124.

Hudak, David E. *Compiling Parallel Loops For High Performance Computers: Partitioning, Data Assignment, And Remapping* ,Boston: Kluwer Academic, 1993, ISBN − 079239283.

Iannucci, Robert A., *Parallel Machines: Parallel Machine Languages: The Emergence Of Hybrid Dataflow Computer Architectures* Boston: Kluwer Academic Publishers, 1990, ASIN 0792391012.

Jacklin, Stephan A.; Leyland, Jane A.;Warmbrodt, William *High-Speed, Automatic Controller Design Consideration for Integrating Array Processor, Multi-*

Microprocessor, and Host Computer System Architecture, NASA/Ames Research Center, Tech Brief ARC-11670, Vol. 11, No. 3.

Jamieson, R. S. *Competitive Parallel Processing for Compression of Data*, R.S. Feb 1990, NASA Tech Brief Vol. 14, No. 2, JPL Invention Report NPO-17445/6952.

Kempster, Linda "Media Madness," 1994. IEEE Mass Storage Model, Version 5.

Henessy, John "Microsupercomputers: Design and Implementation," Stanford University, Computer Systems Laboratory.Semi-annual Tech Report for DARPA, April 1990-Oct. 1990, Contract N00014-87-K-0828.

Hockney, R.W. "Parallel Computation: Architecture, Programming, Algorithms," 1981, Adam Hilger Ltd. ISBN 0-85274-422-6.

Hord, Michael. Parallel Supercomputing in MIMD Architectures, February 1993, ISBN 0-8493-4417-5.

Ido, S. and Hikosawa, S. "Parallel Programming in MIMD type Parallel Systems using Transputer and i860 in Physical Situations," Computational mechanics, 1992 v 10 n 3 / 4 P:151.

Inmos Corp. *Communicating Process Architecture*, 1988, Prentice-Hall, ISBN 0-13-629320-4.

Kalia, R. K. *Toward Teraflop Computing And New Grand Challenge Applications* Commack, N.Y.: Nova Science Publishers, 1995, ASIN: B00A3WCDIW.

Kim, Jong Hyun and E. Pearse O'Grady. "Effect of the Interprocessor Communication Mechanism on Performance of a Parallel Processor System," 1989, IEEE.

Kim, M. "Synchronized Disk Interleaving," Nov. 1986, IEEE Transactions on Computers, V. 55, No. 11, pp 978-988.

Kirk, David B; Hwu, Wen-mei W. *Programming Massively Parallel Processors, Second Edition: A Hands-on Approach,* Morgan Kaufmann; 2nd edition, 2012, ISBN 0124159923.

Kirk, David B; Hwu, Wen-mei W. *Programming Massively Parallel Processors: A Hands-on Approach* (Applications of GPU Computing Series), Morgan Kaufmann; 1st edition, 2010, ISBN-0123814723.

Kishinevsky, Michael; Kondratyev, Alex; Taubin, Alexander; Varshavsky, Victor *Concurrent Hardware: The Theory And Practice Of Self-Timed Design* Chichester; New York: Wiley, 1994, ISBN-0471935360.

Kober, Rudolf *Parallelrechner-Architekturen: Ansatze Fur Imperative Und Deklarative Sprachen*, Berlin; New York: Springer, 1988, ISBN 3540500383.

Kowalik, J. S. (ed) *Parallel Computation And Computers For Artificial Intelligence* Boston: Kluwer Academic Publishers, 1988, ISBN 1461291887.

Kumar, V.K. Prasanna *Parallel Architectures And Algorithms For Image Understanding* / [ed]. Boston : Academic Press, 1991, ISBN-0125640404.

Kung, H. T., "Computational Models for Parallel Computers," Phil. Trans. R. Soc. London, A 326 357-371 (1988).

Lampson. "Hints for Computer System Design," Oct. 1983, ACM Operating Systems Review Vol. 17, No. 5.

Lee, F. and Stiles, G. "Parallel Simulated Annealing: Several Approaches," 1989, NATUG2, IOS Press.

Li, Hungwen; Stout, Quentin F. *Reconfigurable Massively Parallel Computers* Englewood Cliffs, N.J.: Prentice Hall, 1991, ISBN 0137708017.

Lilja, David. "Architectural Alternatives for Exploiting Parallelism," 1991, IEEE Computer Society Press.

Luo, Jenn-Ching. *Parallel Computations on Windows NT*. Baldwin, NY: Parallel Integrated Research, 1995, ISBN-0964436108.

McDonald, Chris. "Teaching Concurrency with Joyce and Linda," SIGCSE bulletin, MAR 01 1992 v 24 n 1 p

46.

McMillin, Bruce M. *Fault Tolerance For Multicomputers: The Application-Oriented Paradigm,* Praeger, 1996, ISBN- 0893918849.

Mendelson, Avi, Mendelson, Bilha. "Toward A General-Purpose Multi-Stream System," Proceedings of the IFIP WG10.3 Working Conference on Parallel Architectures and Compilation Techniques (PACT'94), Montreal, Can, IFIP Transactions A: Computer Science and Technology n A-50 1994.p 335-338 1994 ISSN: 0926-5473.

Miklosko, J. et al (Editor, Contributor) *Algorithms, Software, And Hardware Of Parallel Computers* Berlin; New York: Springer-Verlag; Bratislava: Veda Pub. House of the Slovak Academy of Sciences, 1984, ISBN 366211108X .

Miller, Richard K. *Parallel Processing: The Technology Of Fifth Generation Computer*s Madison, GA: SEAI Technical Publications; Ft. Lee, NJ: Technical Insights, 1985, ASIN 089671067X .

Moore, Fred. "Report on the Development and Evolution of Direct Access Storage Devices 1956-1992 An Update," 1993, Storage Technology Corp. WB9915-A.

Moore, Fred. "Storage The Next Dimension," 10/93, Storage Technology Corp. WB9911-A.

Moore, Fred. "Storage Outlook Making the Connections," 1/95, Storage Technology Corp. WB9911-B.

Morrissey, C. J. "Assignment of Finite Elements to Parallel Processors," Feb. 1990, NASA Tech Brief Vol 14, No. 2, JPL Invention Report NPO-17371/6879.

Moore, Simon W. *Multithreaded Processor Design*, 1996, ISBN-978-0792397182.

Simmons, Margaret L. et al *Debugging And Performance Tuning For Parallel Computing Systems,* Los Alamitos, Calif.: IEEE Computer Society Press, 1996, ISBN-978-0818674129.

Muller, Urs A. *Simulation Of Neural Networks On Parallel Computers* Erste Auflage Konstanz: Hartung-Gorre Verlag, 1993, ISBN-3891916779.

Muntean, T. (ed), Stepney, S. "GRAIL-Graphical Representation of Activity, Interconnection and Loading," 1987, Parallel Programming of Transputer Based Machines, IOS Amsterdam, ISBN-978-9051990072

Murphy, C. G. "Mapping Applications to Architectures," 1989, Research Consortium, Inc., Minneapolis, MN.

Murphy, C. G. "Literature Survey on Tools," SAIC, for NOSC, July 1990, Tech document 1853.

Nicolau, Alexandru (ed) "Advances In Languages And Compilers For Parallel Processing" MIT Press, 1991, Research Monographs In Parallel And Distributed Computing.

Nicolau, Alexandru and Fisher, Joseph A. "Measuring The Parallelism Available For Very Long Instruction Word Architectures," IEEE Transactions on Computers v C-33 n 11 Nov 1984 p 968-976, ISSN: 0018-9340

Nicolau, Alexandru and Fisher, Joseph A. "Using An Oracle To Measure Potential Parallelism In Single Instruction Stream Programs," 14th Annual Microprogramming Workshop, MICRO 14. Conference Location: Chatham, Mass,: 1981 Oct 12-15 MICRO: Annual Microprogramming Workshop 14th. IEEE Computer Society Press (n 373), Los Alamitos, CA, USA, Cat n 81CH1691-5, Piscataway, NJ, p 171-182 1981.

Noble, Bill, Ganz, Rachel, Veer, Bart. "The Helios Parallel Programming Tutorial," 1990, Distributed Software, Ltd.

Pardalos, P. M. (Panos M.), *Topics In Parallel Computing* In Mathematical Programming New York: Science Press, 1992, ISBN-7030033698.

Patterson, D., Garth, G., Katz, R. "A Case for Redundant Arrays of Inexpensive Disks (RAID)," December 1987,

University of California, Berkeley, Report UCB/CSD/87/391.

Pattipati, Kurien, Lee, Luh. "On Mapping a Tracking Algorithm Onto Parallel Processors," Sept 1990, IEEE Transactions on Aerospace and Electronic Systems, Vol. 26, No. 5, Sept 1990.

Perrott, Ronald H. *(ed)Software For Parallel Computers* 1st ed. London; New York: Chapman & Hall, 1992, ISBN-0442314108.

Pfister, Gregory F. In Search Of Clusters: The Coming Battle In Lowly Parallel Computing Upper Saddle River, N.J.: Prentice Hall PTR, 1995.

Philippsen, Michael. Optimierungstechniken Zur Ubersetzung Paralleler Progarammiersprachen Dusseldorf: VDI Verlag, 1994.

Potter, Jerry L. Associative Computing: A Programming Paradigm For Massively Parallel Computers New York: Plenum Press, 1992.

Quinn, Michael J. *Parallel Computing: Theory And Practice* 2nd ed. New York: McGraw-Hill, 1994, ISBN – 0070512949.

Ragsdale, Susan. *Parallel Programming*, 1991, McGraw-Hill, ISBN 0-07-051186-1.

Ramakrishna Rau, B. and Fisher, Joseph A. "Instruction-level Parallel Processing: History, Overview, And Perspective," Journal of Supercomputing v 7 n 1-2 May 1993. p 9-50, SSN: 0920-8542.

Reithinger, Norbert. Eine parallele Architektur zur inkrementellen Generierung multimodaler Dialogbeitrage Sankt Augustin: Infix, 1992.

Rishe, N., Navathe, S., Tal, D. (ed). Parallel Architectures, 1991, IEEE Computer Society Press, ISBN 0-8186-9166-2.

Ruttenberg, John C. and Fisher, Joseph A. "Lifting The Restriction Of Aggregate Data Motion In Parallel Processing," IEEE International Workshop on Computer Systems Organization. New Orleans, La,: 1983 Mar 29-31: IEEE, New York, NY, Cat n 83CH1879-6, Piscataway, NJ, p 211-215, 1983 ISBN: 0-8186-0010-1.

Saghir, Mazen A.R., Chow, Paul, Lee, Corinna G. "Application-Driven Design Of Dsp Architectures And Compilers" Proceedings of the 1994 IEEE International Conference on Acoustics, Speech and Signal Processing. Part 2 (of 6) IEEE, Piscataway, NJ,ISSN: 0736-7791.

Sameh, Ahmed. Linear System Solvers For Parallel Computers Urbana: Dept. of Computer Science, University of Illinois at Urbana- Champaign, 1975.

Samofalov, K. G. Osnovy teorii mnogourovnevykh

konveiernykh vychislitel'nykh sistem, Moskva: "Radio i sviaz'", 1989.

Sapura, David M. "A Parallel Processor Designed for Artificial Neural Systems Simulation," 1990, Loral Space Information Systems.

Schendel, Udo. *Introduction To Numerical Methods For Parallel Computers* Chichester: E. Horwood; New York: Halsted Press, 2nd ed, 1988, ISBN – 085312597X .

Schneck, P. *Supercomputer Architecture*, 1987, Kluwer, ISBN 0-89838-238-6.

Scientific American, *Trends in Computing*, 1988, Vol. 1.

Seery, et al."System-Level Strategy Attacks Key Multiuser Bottlenecks," Jan. 1, 1988, Computer Design.

Shekhar, K.H. and Srikant, Y.N. "Linda Sub System on Transputers," Computer Languages, 1993 v 18 n 2 P 125.

Shiva, Sajjan G. *Pipelined And Parallel Computer Architectures* New York, NY: Harper Collins College Publishers, 1997, ISBN- 0673520935.

Simmons, Margaret; Ingrid Bucher, Ingrid; Koskela, Rebecca (Ed) *Instrumentation For Future Parallel Computing Systems* New York, N.Y.: ACM Press; Addison-Wesley, Advanced Book Program, 1989, ISBN 0201503905.

Sittig, D.F., Shifman, M.A., Nadkarni, P. "Parallel Computation for Medicine and Biology: Applications of Linda at Yale University," The International Journal of Supercomputer Applications, Summer 1992 v 6 n 2 P 147.

Snyder, Lawrence *Algorithmically Specialized Parallel Computers* Orlando: Academic Press, 1985, ISBN-0126541302.

Soucek, Branko. *Neural And Massively Parallel Computers: The Sixth Generation* New York: Wiley, 1989, ISBN 0471508896.

Stakem, Patrick H. "The Brilliant Bulldozer: Parallel Processing Techniques for Onboard Computation in Unmanned Vehicles," 1988, presented at 15th AUVS Symposium, San Diego, Ca. June 6-8, 1988.

Stakem, Pattick H. *Multicore Computer Architecture*, May, 2014, PRRB Publishing, ASIN B00KB2XIQ0.

Stakem, Patrick H. *The Architecture and Applications of the ARM Microprocessors* (Computer Architecture Book 7), February 2013, PRRB Publishing, ASIN B00BAFF4OQ.

Stakem, Patrick H. *RISC Microprocessors, History and Overview* (Computer Architecture Book 3) June 2013, PRRB Publishing, ASIN B00D5SCHQO.

Stakem, Patrick H. *A Practitioner's Guide to RISC Microprocessor Architecture*, 1st ed, 1996, Wiley-Interscience, ISBN 0471130184

Stepney, S. "GRAIL - Graphical Representation of Activity, Interconnection and Loading," Parallel Programming of Transputer Based Machines, Muntean, T. (ed), 1987, IOS Amsterdam.

Sterling, Thomas, Messina, Paul, Smith, Paul H. "Enabling Technologies for Peta(FL)OPS Computing," July, 1994, CCSF-45, Caltech Concurrent Supercomputing Facility, Caltech.

Swan, R., Fuller, S., Siewiorek, D. "Cm* - A Modula, Multi-microprocessor," P. AFIPS, 1977 Fall JCC, pps. 637-644.

Treleaven, P. (Author); Vanneschi M. (Ed) *Future Parallel Computers: An Advanced Course*, Pisa, Italy, June 9-10, 1986: Proceedings Berlin; New York: Springer-Verlag, 1987, ISBN 0387182039.

Treleaven, Philip C. *Parallel Computers: Object-Oriented, Functional, Logic*, Chichester, West Sussex, England; New York, NY, USA: Wiley, 1990, ASIN 0471925187.

Trew, Arthur; Wilson, Greg *Past, Present, Parallel: A Survey Of Available Parallel Computer Systems* London;

New York: Springer-Verlag, 1991, ISBN 3540196641.

Tseng, Emy, Reiner, David. "Parallel Database Processing on the KSR1 Computer," ACM SIGMOD International Conference on Management of Data, May 25-28, 1993.

Udiavar, Nandan, and Styles, G. S. "A Simple but Flexible Model for Determining Optimal Task Allocation and Configuration on a Network of Transputers," 1989, Transputer Research and Applications 1, IOS, ISBN 90-5199-026-X.

Uhr, Leonard *Parallel Computer Vision*, 1987, Boston: Academic Press, ISBN 0124333109.

Vernon, David, *Parallel Computer Vision: the Vis a Vis system* New York: Ellis Horwood Ltd, 1992, ISBN-0139327169.

Weichslgartner, Andreas Stefan, Wildermann, Stephan

Invasive Computing for Mapping Parallel Programs to Many-Core Architectures (Computer Architecture and Design Methodologies) Weichslgartner,Stefan Wildermann, et al. 2017, et al

Wijshoff, Harry A. G., *Data Organization In Parallel Computers,* Boston: Kluwer Academic Publishers, 1989, ISBN-978-0898383041.

Williams, S. *Programming Models for Parallel Systems*,

1990, Wiley, ISBN 0-471-92304-4.

Wulf, William A. Bell, C. Gordon. "C.mmp - A Multi-miniprocessor," P. AFIPS, 1972 Fall JCC, 41, pps. 765-777.

Xu, Cheng-Zhong, Lau, Francis C.M. *Load Balancing In Parallel Computers: Theory And Practice*, 1997, Kluwer Academic Publishers, ISBN-978-079239196.

Selected Papers and Proceedings

"Parallelism in the Instruction Pipeline," Dec 1989, High Performance Systems.

"Multiple Chips Speed CPU Performance," Sept. 1989, High Performance Systems.

"Six Case Studies Of Real Machines," Jan 1989, IEEE Computer.

"Turn a PC into a Supercomputer with Plug-In Boards," 1988, Electronic Design.

"System-Level Strategy Attacks Key Multiuser Bottlenecks," January 1988,Computer Design.
Nussbaum, Daniel and Anant Agarwal. "Scalability of Parallel Machines," March 1991, CACM, Vol. 34, No. 3.

"Proceedings of 19xx International Conference on

Parallel Processing," Pennsylvania State University Press (avail. 1976-1996).

Proceedings of the Institute of Electrical and Electronics Engineers, April 1991, Special Issue on Massively Parallel Computers.

"Grand Challenges: High Performance Computing and Communications," 1991, A report by the Committee on Physical, Mathematical, and Engineering Sciences, National Science Foundation.

Proceedings, Scalable High Performance Computing Conference, SHPCC-92, April 26-29, 1992, Williamsburg, Va. IEEE Computer Society.

"Proceedings of the Fifth IEEE Symposium on Parallel and Distributed Processing," 1993, IEEE Computer Society Press, ISBN 0-8186-4222-X.

"Proceedings of the 1993 International Conference on Parallel Processing," 1993, CRC Press, ISBN 0-8493-8983-6 (in 3 volumes).

Astfalk, Greg. "Fundamentals and Practicalities of MPP," July 1993, Convex Computer.

Symmetry Multiprocessor Architecture Overview, 1003-50113-03, Sequent Computer Systems, Inc. 1994.

Kendall Square Research Technical Summary, 1992,

Kendall Square Research.

Convex Exemplar Architecture, 1993, DHW-014, Convex Computer Corp.

Proceedings, Scalable High Performance Computing Conference, SHPCC-92, April 26-29, 1992, Williamsburg, Va. IEEE Computer Society.

"Massively Parallel System Delivers 68,500 MIPS," Electronic Design. Oct. 15 1992 v 40 n 21 Page: 89.

"Memory Multicomputer Architecture," <u>Computer</u>, Feb 01 1991 v 24 n 2 p 33.

An Automatic Parallelizing Converter: BERT, A. Bogatov, K. Eliseev, V. Rychkov, ECSC MIPT 9, Institutski per., Dolgoprydny, Moscow region, 141700, Russia, P. Telegin, Institute of Cybernetic Problems, Academy Sci. of Russia, 37, Vavilova st., Moscow, Russia.

"Zephyr, A tool for Parallel Computing," Reference Manual Excerpts, Paralogic, 9/30/92.

"BERT MIMD Parallel Compiler for Fortran 77," Technical Overview, Paralogic, 1992.

"i860 Parallel Programming System," The i860 Toolset, Transtech Parallel Systems, July, 1992.

iWarp Microprocessor, Intel, 1991, order 318153.

iWarp Programmers Guide, Intel, 318151.

iWarp Users Guide, Intel, 318158.

Introduction to iWARP, Intel, 318150.

Supporting Systolic and Memory Communication in iWARP, IEEE.

Fried, Stephen S. "i860 Software Performance Considerations," Microway Corp.

Stevens, R.S. "Distributed Memory Multi-Processing with the Intel i860," presented at NATUG-93.

"Beyond Vectorizing Compilers The Standard Math Library," Jan. 1993, Sky Computers Tech Brief.

"Managing I/O And Computation," Jan. 1993, Sky Computers Tech Brief.

"The Case for RAID," U. C. Berkeley, Computer Science Department, Dec. 1987.

"Hard Disk Drives: Technology Overview," July 1994, Datapro, McGraw-Hill.

"Disk Array Storage Subsystems: Overview," January 1994, Datapro, McGraw-Hill.

"Proceedings of 19xx International Conference on Parallel Processing," Pennsylvania State University Press. (series)

Proceedings of the Institute of Electrical and Electronics Engineers, April 1991, Special Issue on Massively Parallel Computers

"Grand Challenges: High Performance Computing and Communications," A report by the Committee on Physical, Mathematical, and Engineering Sciences, NSF, 1991.

Gardner III, Dr. George O. "The Evolution of Parallel Processing," Beyond Computing, May/June 1994, pp 22-26.

Supercomputers And Parallel Computation: based on the proceedings of a workshop on progress in the use of vector and array processors Oxford [Oxfordshire]: Clarendon Press; New York: Oxford University Press, 1984.

IMACS World Congress on Systems Simulation and Scientific Computation (10th: 1982: Montreal, Quebec) Parallel and large-scale computers: performance, architecture, applications, New York: Elsevier Science Pub. Co., 1983.

Fourth NASA Goddard Conference on Mass Storage Systems and Technologies, NASA Conference

Publications, 1995.

"What's the Disk-Drive Interface Of The Future?," April 1995, OEM Magazine, Vol. 3., No. 16, pp 12-13.

Parallel Computing On Distributed Memory Multiprocessors edited by Fusun Ozguner, Fikret Ercal. Berlin; New York: Springer-Verlag, c1993, Proceedings of the NATO Advanced Study Institute on Parallel Computing on Distributed Memory Multiprocessors, held at Bilkent University, Ankara, Turkey, July 1-13, 1991.

Software For Parallel Computation edited by Janusz S. Kowalik, Lucio Grandinetti. New York : Springer-Verlag, 1993, Proceedings of the NATO Advanced Research Workshop on Software for Parallel Computation, Cetraro, Cosenza, Italy, June 22-26, 1992.

Cray T3D Massively Parallel Processing System [videorecording /] Steve Nelson, Steve Oberlin. Stanford, CA : University Video Communications, 1993 1 videocassette (57 min.) 1/2 in. The Distinguished Lecture Series: Leaders In Computer Science And Electrical Engineering. Presentation Recorded August 26, 1993. Sponsored by Cray Research, Inc.

Proceedings EuroPVM '96 (1996: Munchen, Germany) Parallel Virtual Machine, Third European PVM Conference, Munchen, Germany, October 7-9, 1996 Berlin; New York: Springer.

"1995 Programming Models For Massively Parallel Computers," proceedings, October 9-12, 1995, Berlin, Germany Los Alamitos, Calif. IEEE Computer Society Press, 1995.

Proceedings of 1994 IEEE Region 10's Ninth Annual International Conference: Frontiers Of Computer Technology, 22-26 August, 1994, Singapore [New York]: Institute of Electrical and Electronics Engineers, 1994.

IFIP WG10.3 Working Conference on Parallel Architectures and Compilation Techniques (1994: Montreal, Canada) proceedings of the IFIP WG10.3 Working Conference on Parallel Architectures and Compilation Techniques, PACT ' 94, Montreal, Canada, 24-26 August, 1994 Amsterdam, The Netherlands; New York: North-Holland, 1994.

PCRCW '94 (1994: Seattle, Wash.) Parallel Computer Routing And Communication: First International Workshop, PCRCW '94, Seattle, Washington, USA, May 16-18, 1994: proceedings Berlin; New York: Springer-Verlag, 1994.

Emerging Trends In Database And Knowledge-Base Machines: The Application Of Parallel Architectures To Smart Information Systems Los Alamitos, CA: IEEE Computer Society Press, 1995.

Interconnection Networks For High-Performance Parallel

Computers Los Alamitos, Calif.: IEEE Computer Society Press, 1994.

Programming Models For Massively Parallel Computers, 1993: Proceedings, September 20-23, 1993, Berlin, Germany Los Alamitos, Calif.: IEEE Computer Society Press, 1993.

Nixdorf Symposium Parallel Architectures And Their Efficient Use: First Heinz Nixdorf Symposium, Paderborn, Germany, November 11-13, 1992: proceedings Berlin; New York: Springer-Verlag, 1993.

IFIP WG 10.3 Working Conference on Architectures and Compilation Techniques for Fine and Medium Grain Parallelism (1993: Orlando, Fla.) Proceedings of the IFIP WG 10.3 Working Conference on Architectures and Compilation Techniques for Fine and Medium Grain Parallelism, Orlando, Florida, USA, 20-22 January 1993 Amsterdam; New York: North-Holland, 1993.

Workshop on Performance Measurement and Visualization (1992: Moravany and Vahom, Czechoslovakia), Moravany, Czechoslovakia, 23-24 October 1992 Amsterdam; New York: North-Holland, 1993.

Conference on Parallel Architectures and Languages Europe (1991: Eindhoven, Netherlands) PARLE '91: Parallel Architectures And Languages Europe Berlin; New York: Springer-Verlag, 1991.

Parallel Architectures And Neural Networks: third Italian workshop, Vietri sul Mare, Salerno, 15-18 May, 1990 Singapore; Teaneck, N.J.: World Scientific, 1990.

US/Japan Workshop on Parallel Lisp (1989: Sendai-shi, Miyagi-ken, Japan) Parallel Lisp: Languages And Systems: US/Japan Workshop on Parallel Lisp, Sendai, Japan, June 5-8, 1989, proceedings Berlin; New York: Springer-Verlag, 1990.

Architectural Alternatives For Exploiting Parallelism Los Alamitos, Calif.: IEEE Computer Society Press, 1991.

Parallel Architectures And Neural Networks: fourth Italian workshop, Vietri sul Mare, Salerno, 8-10 May 1991 Singapore; River Edge, N.J.: World Scientific, 1991.

Parallel Architectures For Image Processing: 14-15 February 1990, Santa Clara, California Bellingham, Wash., USA: The Society, 1990.

IFIP WG 10.3 Working Conference on Highly Parallel Computers for Numerical and Signal Processing Applications 1986: Sophia-Antipolis, France, Proceedings of the IFIP WG 10.3 Working Conference on Highly Parallel Computers for Numerical and Signal Processing Applications, Elsevier Science Pub. Co., 1987.

Structures Congress '86 (1986: New Orleans, La.) Super And Parallel Computers And Their Impact On Civil Engineering: Proceedings Of A Session At Structures Congress '86, Hyatt Regency Hotel, New Orleans, Louisiana, September 15-18, 1986 New York, N.Y.: The Society, 1986.

American Society of Mechanical Engineers. Winter Meeting (1987: Boston, Mass.) Parallel Computations And Their Impact On Mechanics New York,: ASME, 1987.

Parallel Computers--Parallel Mathematics: Proceedings Of The IMACS (AICA)-GI Symposium, March 14-16, 1977, Technical University of Munich Amsterdam; New York: North-Holland Pub. Co. New York, American Elsevier Pub. Co., 1977.

International PARLE Conference (4th: 1992: Paris, France) PARLE '92, Parallel Architectures And Languages Europe: 4th International PARLE Conference, Paris, France, June 15-18, 1992, proceedings Berlin; New York: Springer-Verlag, 1992.

MPMS in Japan

This section summarizes the work in massively parallel microprocessor based systems going on in Japan. The major players are the three Japanese Supercomputer vendors: NEC, Hitachi, and Fujitsu. Generally, their products are not available in North America.

Fujitsu has sought high performance from Gallium Arsenide chips, and has maintained chip fab facilities for several RISC architectures. Their own machines include the Fujitsu AP1000 machine, and the VPP500 series. They maintain a research facility, The Fujitsu Parallel Computing Laboratory, in Japan.

Hitachi has long been in the IBM-compatible mainframe market, but has now seen the value and interest in massively parallel machines. They use the HP-PA chipset, and plan to couple several thousand of these. Several other projects are also ongoing, one of which involves the PowerPC chip, linked on the PCI bus.

NEC's Cenju-3 machine utilizes the MIPS R4400 chip, and runs the Japanese language variant of Unix, EWS UX. SX-3R series. NEC's planned machine will use 32 processors in a box, with the capability of clustering up to 16 boxes.

JTEC/WTEC Annual Reports.

204

Spacecraft Supercomputer

This work was supported in part by NASA under Contract NAS5-31409 during the period January to June, 1991.

The goal of this effort was to define an architecture with an order of magnitude performance increase over existing spacecraft onboard computing resources. This goal was exceeded, by exploiting scalable parallel architectures.

This effort established the feasibility of using off-the-shelf hardware with a known path to full space qualification to address a large set of user processing needs in the area of sensed data sets for Earth Observation, including weather, data. It is no longer feasible to collect large volumes of data that are downlinked over already strained communication channels to large central archive and processing centers based on old-generation computational resources. Now, the choice is between not collecting the data versus generating useful data products close to the data source, and directly downlinking these to users in the field, in addition to and in parallel with the classical data collection and downlink tasks. In many cases, the user's needs are for the receipt of timely data products directly at a remote site. This is not cost effective or even feasible for most current or planned data processing facilities for downlinked sensed data.

One major focus of the High Performance Computing and Communications (HPCC) Program is "in making parallel computing easier to use and scalable..." NASA's role in HPCC is "to accelerate the development and application of high performance computing technologies to meet NASA's science and engineering requirements." This applies to NASA's ground based systems, and also to flight systems, which lag further and further behind. Application of these techniques involve a major effort in system design. The application of new architectures involve the development of new toolsets, software, and paradigms.

This effort focused on extracting information from raw data onboard the spacecraft at the sensor, and established the feasibility of generating data products onboard for direct downlink in a timely manner by using proven hardware, architecture, and algorithms. This approach does not preclude or interfere with the normal collection and archiving of sensed data, but rather works with data tapped off the main stream, and processed in a parallel stream.

Scalable parallel processing techniques are applicable to a large set of spacecraft onboard processing tasks now and in the immediate future. This application will provide the capability to generate and rapidly distribute data products that cannot otherwise be done.

At the time, the Transputer was seen as the best candidate for implementation of this approach. The Transputer is supported by an Ada compiler from Alsys Corp, as well as numerous other languages with parallel extensions.

Although the goal of this study was to define an architecture with an order of magnitude performance increase over existing onboard computing resources, it was shown that several orders of magnitude were feasible. With scalable processor/communication resources, the hardware can be more appropriately matched to the problem domain, while retaining redundancy and reprogrammability.

The early phases of the study identified a series of candidate science payloads or instruments that the Flight Supercomputer can provide services to. The key goal in this phase was to identify a real application that can be implemented without impacting the instrument schedule or mission success, but that would allow the collection of data that would otherwise be lost. An observing class instrument was preferred, as it would provide a large data source.

Requirements for throughput and processing were derived from EOS instruments-class data. These data provided a strawman set of requirements. Numerous applications were found that could benefit from the utilization of parallel processor technology. These all revolved around the onboard generation and direct downlink of data products of a local interest in a timely fashion to end users in the field. In most cases, the timeliness issue precluded the downlink of data to a classical ground processing facility for data product generation, followed by a dissemination, possible by re-uplink and rebroadcast. The complexity of the onboard system interacts with the complexity, and thus cost, of the ground station equipment. This introduced the concepts of data compression/decompression for transmission. The ground receiving station, exclusive of the RF portion, was considered to be a laptop class computer, augmented with a front-end processor, probably based on a complementary scalable parallel processor. This front-end processor would be a custom designed box. In most cases, the ground based application would be cost sensitive.

Space Computer Corp.

Space Computer Corp. of California was under contract to DARPA to produce a "Miniaturized, Low-Power Parallel Processor". Their approach has been to use the Transputer as a communication element for Vector co-processors. A prototype system for guided missile applications was delivered in April 1990, and provided a peak processing throughput of 1.3 Gflops. Current efforts focus on microminiaturization of the technology, using custom designed ASIC's and wafer scale integration.

The applications for the resulting device include sensor image processing, and Synthetic aperture radar (SAR) processing, including image compression tasks. The SCC-100 is a multi-node device, with each node consisting of a Transputer, memory, and Zoran vector signal processor chips. The Zoran chips provide the computational throughput, and the Transputers provide communications and control. Flight units will require the availability of rad-hard, Mil-spec die.

Earth Sciences Observations (EOS)Applications

This section discusses the potential application of the Flight Supercomputer to data processing requirements derived from Earth observing class spacecraft, including weather satellites.

The Earth Observation Satellite platforms will have two direct broadcast channels, 1 supporting a 15 Mbps rate, and the other supporting 100 mbps. The high rate channel is nominally dedicated to 1 instrument, but can provide a backup to the nominal TDRSS high rate link. The EOS platform instrument set is still not completely defined, but a representative set was used to determine if the Transputer link I/O was capable of supporting the collection of data. Processing of data was not considered, since the algorithms were yet undefined.

In all cases, the data input capacity of a single link on the T-800 transputer is sufficient to handle the average data rate of the instrument. A single link is also sufficient for the peak rate for all but the HIRIS and ITIR. With 4 links, the transputer can input more than 1 instrument stream continuously, and with external multiplexing, can handle the entire instrument set. Using data from the an early EOS-A instrument set, the instruments' data could be handled by a T-800 transputer link, with the exception of the HIRIS instrument in peak mode, which outputted data at 160 Mbps. The EOS instrument-derived requirements enveloped the instrument data rates for Earth observing missions in the near future.

Wildfire Mapping, Oil Slicks, and Schools of Fish

Numerous applications exist in the field of Earth Resources mapping, particularly where asynchronous events directly affect human activities, or require timely response. In many cases, the required data product calculation and distribution must be performed at the data source. This implies the capability of onboard processing of sensed data, and direct downlink of the resultant data products, in parallel with the normal data downlink. It is anticipated that several algorithms could reside in onboard memory, and that code could be uplinked rapidly to implement new or modified algorithms in response to unanticipated events.

One potential data product for onboard calculation involves the determination of the perimeter of a forest fire, which is a classic edge-detection problem, given a thermal band image. Direct downlink to the forest fire command center is essential for freshness of the data. The on-site equipment must be small, lightweight, and inexpensive, so that it can be air-dropped and abandoned if necessary.

The data products of interest to the fire management crews on the ground include the flame front location, direction and rate of spread, smoke plume dimension, and hot spot detection. These data were used for personnel and equipment placement and logistics and safety. Observations from U-2 aircraft as well as TIROS series weather satellites have been used to gather relevant data on fires.

Perimeter determination can be accomplished with a Laplacian operator, which is homogeneous. This is followed by a scaling, a full rectification, and a thresholding. This can be done on 1 Transputer at the data rate. The onboard data storage requirements can be minimized by clever organization of the algorithm. Data storage is a premium item that must be minimized for space flight use. Not only are the storage devices expensive, but they consume resources such as size, weight, and onboard power.

Similar to the determination of the perimeter of a fire is the determination of the area of an oil slick on a body of water. In this case we are interested in the perimeter, but can determine the extent of the "blob", and track the shape, location, and drift. Downlink data can be sent directly to the site, and used to position containment equipment. The oil slick identification problem maps easily to the problem of determining the extend of the spread of floodwaters.

Another related problem is the timely determination of

the location of schools of fish near the continental shelves, using ocean colorimetery. This process is of interest to commercial fishing fleets, and the timeliness of the information is essential, requiring direct downlink to fishing fleets. Cost of the fleet equipment is also an issue.

Similar applications involve specialized operations to image active volcanoes, or to locate and track the eye of severe storms (hurricanes or typhoons). All of these processes are classical image processing applications that can be hosted on one or several Transputers. In most cases the core algorithm is less than 100 lines of code, but is applied across a real time data set. In this case, a systolic pipeline of Transputers may be the ideal topology.

Wind Vector Derivation

Using successive images of cloud formations, properly registered by visible land mass, the wind vectors may be inferred by cloud motion. This process involves multi-spectral imaging (visible and infrared) from spacecraft such as SMS and GOES. The derived wind information is of importance in global weather pattern understanding and prediction, and is critical to severe storm forecasting. Implementing this process onboard will result in the ability to generate an downlink a data product that is of timely interest.

The required derivation of the data on the ground has

been difficult and time-consuming, and has not been available operationally. The algorithms described in the literature postulate quasi-real time implementation on superminicomputers augmented with array processors. This process could also be implemented on arrays of Transputers, and may be the most promising candidate for further implementation.

Alternate Architectures

This section discusses that part of the study that looked at the initial assumption of using the Transputer, to see if that was still valid in the light of advancing technology, and product announcements from other vendors, as well as advances from Inmos.

A number of alternate computer and connectivity architectures for the flight supercomputer were examined to establish a taxonomy of choices and grade these according to the realities of schedule and availability. Existing and emerging RISC chips such as the MIPS R3000, the Intel i80860 and 960, the Motorola 96000 DSP series, etc. were examined to determine if there was a better alternative to the Transputer chip, before committing to a processor choice. Of concern were availability, vendor support, and software development tools.

No processor could be found that could provide the same level of connectivity as the Transputer, and the Transputer was ahead in terms of Processor-I/O balance. The current unavailability of the unit in space-qualified versions is the only drawback. The closest second candidate was the recently announced Texas Instruments 'C40 Parallel DSP, which is marketed as a DSP, not a general purpose computer. Because TI has a history of developing Military versions of its products, it is worthwhile to continue to track its development. The communication architecture of the C40 uses parallel ports with dma engines, and is necessarily distance-limited. Data on the '040 only recently became available, and it was not possible to completely evaluate it for the purposes of this study. No other architecture could be found that provided the Transputer's inherent communication capability and connectivity, without extensive glue-logic. In fact, many emerging systems use the transputer as a communication element for fast RISC processors such as Intel's i860 or Motorola 96000 series. The remainder of this section discusses some of the other RISC architectures that were examined.

The R3000 and Intel 80960 family were selected for the 32-bit follow-on to the 1750A architecture for military avionics by the JIAWG. However, neither provide a connectivity solution comparable to the transputer. The i80386 is being qualified for use on the Space Station Freedom and with the Flight Telerobotic Servicer, but that chip is not designed for multiprocessing.

As with any space application, the usability of parts will lag the commercial state of the art by 3-10 years. Any new architecture suggested must be available in the correct package, and available with the applicable process screening.

Examining the general problem domain for onboard processing of sensed data, the full spectrum from matrix multiplication (compute-bound) to matrix addition (I/O bound) is seen. Compute bound processes can always be speeded up by faster computational components, faster memory, or a smarter architecture. I/O bound problems present a greater challenge. In fact, it is relatively easy to transform a compute bound problem to an I/O bound problem with a parallel processor. One solution, studied at Carnegie-Mellon University, is the systolic processor, which is a matrix of simple, interconnected processor elements with I/O at the boundaries, and a pipelined processing approach to data that is pulsed through the array. In this scheme (since instantiated in the iWarp product, by Intel), multiple use can be made of each data item, and a high throughput can be achieved with modest I/O rate. There is extensive concurrency and modular expand-ability, and the control and data flow are simple and regular. This technique, easily implemented on Transputers, lends itself well to repetitive operations on large data sets, such as those generated by spaceborne sensors.

Scaleable systems, those made up of multiple computational/communication building blocks, have an architecture that is responsive to the problem domain. In such a homogeneous system, the correct amount of processing and I/O can be provided for the initial requirements, with the ability to expand later in a building block fashion to address evolved requirements as well as redundancy or fault tolerance. Developing software for scaleable systems is a challenge, mostly in deciding how the software is spread across the computational nodes. This is a solvable problem, based both on good software tools and on programmer experience. Research into these topics, as well as the ability of the system itself to adapt to processing load, is ongoing.

Of course, the applicability of the parallel processor to a given problem set implies that the applicable algorithm can be parallelized, and a solution can be implemented and debugged in a reasonable time. This implies that an efficient programming and debugging environment exist for the selected hardware. This is certainly the case for Transputer-based systems. The major hurdle is conceptual for the systems integrators - the ability to think in parallel paradigms. This comes with hands-on experience.

Bibliography

"Miniaturized, Low-Power Parallel Processor Technology (Advanced Space Technology Program) Status Briefing," 26 March 1991, Space Computer Corp.

Schwalb, Arthur. "The Tiros-N/NOAA A-G Satellite Series," NOAA Tech Memo NESS 95, Aug. 1979.

"Aircraft and Satellite Thermographic Systems for Wildfire Mapping and Assessment," J. A. Brass, V.G.

Ambrosia, P.J. Riggan, J.S. Myers, J.C. Arvesen, AIAA paper AIAA-87-0187.

"Automated Mesoscale Winds Derived from Goes Multispectral Imagery," Robert J. Atkinson (GE), Gregory S. Wilson (NASA/MSFC), (unpublished).

"Design Considerations for EOS Direct Broadcast," Charles H. Vermillion (GSFC), Paul H. Chan (SSAI), 1991.

"Data Volumes and Assumptions," EOSDIS Core System Requirement Specification, 14 Sept, 1990, NASA/GSFC.

wikipedia, various.

Trademarks

The following trademarks, listed in alphabetical order, are the property of the respective owners.

Ada	U.S. Government, Ada Joint Program Office
Alpha AXP	Digital Equipment Corp.
Am 29000	Advanced Micro Devices Inc.
Am29027	Advanced Micro Devices Inc.
AMD	Advanced Micro Devices Inc.
ASM29K	Microtek Research, Inc.
Centronics	Centronics Data Computer Corp.
CLIPPER	Intergraph Corp.
CRAY	Cray Research Inc.
CRAY Y-MP	Digital Equipment Corp.
DEC	Digital Equipment Corp.
Ethernet	Xerox Crop.
Embedded System Processor	National Semiconductor
GIGAswitch	Digital Equipment Corp.
i286	Intel Corp.
i386	Intel Corp.
i387	Intel Corp.
i486	Intel Corp.
i750	Intel Corp.
i860	Intel Corp.
i960	Intel Corp.
iAPX	Intel Corp.
IBM	International Business Machines Corp.

IBM PC	International Business Machines Corp.
ICE	Intel Corp.
IMS	Inmos Group
inmos	Inmos Group
INTEL	Intel Corp.
Intergraph	Intergraph Corp.
iWARP	Intel Corp.
LOTUS	Lotus Development Corp.
MasPar	MasPar Computer Corp.
MC 68000	Motorola
Microsoft	Microsoft Corporation
Motorola	Motorola
Motorola 88100	Motorola
Multibus	Intel Corp.
NFS	Sun Microsystems, Inc.
Occam	Inmos Group
OSF/1	Open Software Foundation, Inc.
PARC	Xerox Corp.
PDP-11	Digital Equipment Corp.
Pentium	Intel Corp.
PIC	Microchip Technology
POSIX	IEEE
PowerPC	InternationalBusiness Machines
PowerPC Architecture	InternationalBusiness Machines
PowerPC 601	InternationalBusiness Machines
RISCompiler	MIPS Computer Systems Inc.
RISCwindows	MIPS Computer Systems Inc.
RS/6000	International BusinessMachines
Solaris	SunSoft
SPARC	SPARC International

SPARClite	SPARC International
Sun	Sun Microsystems, Inc
SuperSPARC	Texas Instruments
Tandem	Tandem Computers, Inc.
TI	Texas Instruments
UNIX	UNIX Systems Laboratories
VAX	Digital Equipment Corp.
VMS	Digital Equipment Corp.
Windows	Microsoft Corp.
Windows NT	Microsoft Corp.
WordPerfect	WordPerfect Corp.
X Windows System	MIT

If you enjoyed this book, you might also be interested in some of these.

16-bit Microprocessors, History and Architecture, 2013 PRRB Publishing, ISBN-1520210922.

4- and 8-bit Microprocessors, Architecture and History, 2013, PRRB Publishing, ISBN-152021572X,

Apollo's Computers, 2014, PRRB Publishing, ISBN-1520215800.

The Architecture and Applications of the ARM Microprocessors, 2013, PRRB Publishing, ISBN-1520215843.

Earth Rovers: for Exploration and Environmental Monitoring, 2014, PRRB Publishing, ISBN-152021586X.

Embedded Computer Systems, Volume 1, Introduction and Architecture, 2013, PRRB Publishing, ISBN-1520215959.

The History of Spacecraft Computers from the V-2 to the Space Station, 2013, PRRB Publishing, ISBN-1520216181.

Floating Point Computation, 2013, PRRB Publishing, ISBN-152021619X.

Architecture of Massively Parallel Microprocessor Systems, 2011, PRRB Publishing, ISBN-1520250061.

Multicore Computer Architecture, 2014, PRRB Publishing, ISBN-1520241372.

Personal Robots, 2014, PRRB Publishing, ISBN-1520216254.

RISC Microprocessors, History and Overview, 2013, PRRB Publishing, ISBN-1520216289.

*Robots and Telerobots in Space Application*s, 2011, PRRB Publishing, ISBN-1520210361.

The Saturn Rocket and the Pegasus Missions, 1965, 2013, PRRB Publishing, ISBN-1520209916.

Visiting the NASA Centers, and Locations of Historic Rockets & Spacecraft, 2017, PRRB Publishing, ISBN-1549651205.

Microprocessors in Space, 2011, PRRB Publishing, ISBN-1520216343.

Computer *Virtualization and the Cloud*, 2013, PRRB Publishing, ISBN-152021636X.

What's the Worst That Could Happen? Bad Assumptions, Ignorance, Failures and Screw-ups in Engineering Projects, 2014, PRRB Publishing, ISBN-1520207166.

Computer Architecture & Programming of the Intel x86 Family, 2013, PRRB Publishing, ISBN-1520263724.

The Hardware and Software Architecture of the Transputer, 2011,PRRB Publishing, ISBN-152020681X.

Mainframes, Computing on Big Iron, 2015, PRRB Publishing, ISBN- 1520216459.

Spacecraft Control Centers, 2015, PRRB Publishing, ISBN-1520200617.

Embedded in Space, 2015, PRRB Publishing, ISBN-1520215916.

A Practitioner's Guide to RISC Microprocessor Architecture, Wiley-Interscience, 1996, ISBN-0471130184.

Cubesat Engineering, PRRB Publishing, 2017, ISBN-1520754019.

Cubesat Operations, PRRB Publishing, 2017, ISBN-152076717X.

Interplanetary Cubesats, PRRB Publishing, 2017, ISBN-1520766173 .

Cubesat Constellations, Clusters, and Swarms, Stakem, PRRB Publishing, 2017, ISBN-1520767544.

Graphics Processing Units, an overview, 2017, PRRB Publishing, ISBN-1520879695.

Intel Embedded and the Arduino-101, 2017, PRRB Publishing, ISBN-1520879296.

Orbital Debris, the problem and the mitigation, 2018, PRRB Publishing, ISBN-*1980466483.*

Manufacturing in Space, 2018, PRRB Publishing, ISBN-1977076041.

NASA's Ships and Planes, 2018, PRRB Publishing, ISBN-1977076823.

Space Tourism, 2018, PRRB Publishing, ISBN-1977073506.

STEM – Data Storage and Communications, 2018, PRRB Publishing, ISBN-1977073115.

In-Space Robotic Repair and Servicing, 2018, PRRB Publishing, ISBN-1980478236.

Introducing Weather in the pre-K to 12 Curricula, A Resource Guide for Educators, 2017, PRRB Publishing, ISBN-1980638241.

Introducing Astronomy in the pre-K to 12 Curricula, A Resource Guide for Educators, 2017, PRRB Publishing,

ISBN-198104065X.
Also available in a Brazilian Portuguese edition, ISBN-1983106127.

Deep Space Gateways, the Moon and Beyond, 2017, PRRB Publishing, ISBN-1973465701.

Exploration of the Gas Giants, Space Missions to Jupiter, Saturn, Uranus, and Neptune, PRRB Publishing, 2018, ISBN-9781717814500.

Crewed Spacecraft, 2017, PRRB Publishing, ISBN-1549992406.

Rocketplanes to Space, 2017, PRRB Publishing, ISBN-1549992589.

Crewed Space Stations, 2017, PRRB Publishing, ISBN-1549992228.

Enviro-bots for STEM: Using Robotics in the pre-K to 12 Curricula, A Resource Guide for Educators, 2017, PRRB Publishing, ISBN-1549656619.

STEM-Sat, Using Cubesats in the pre-K to 12 Curricula, A Resource Guide for Educators, 2017, ISBN-1549656376.

Embedded GPU's, 2018, PRRB Publishing, ISBN-1980476497.

Mobile Cloud Robotics, 2018, PRRB Publishing, ISBN-1980488088.

Extreme Environment Embedded Systems, 2017, PRRB Publishing, ISBN-1520215967.

What's the Worst, Volume-2, 2018, ISBN-1981005579.

Spaceports, 2018, ISBN-1981022287.

Space Launch Vehicles, 2018, ISBN-1983071773.

Mars, 2018, ISBN-1983116902.

X-86, 40ᵗʰ Anniversary ed, 2018, ISBN-1983189405.

Lunar Orbital Platform-Gateway, 2018, PRRB Publishing, ISBN-1980498628.

Space Weather, 2018, ISBN-1723904023.

STEM-Engineering Process, 2017, ISBN-1983196517.

Space Telescopes, 2018, PRRB Publishing, ISBN-1728728568.

Exoplanets, 2018, PRRB Publishing, ISBN-9781731385055.

Planetary Defense, 2018, PRRB Publishing, ISBN-9781731001207.

Exploration of the Asteroid Belt, 2018, PRRB Publishing, ISBN-1731049846.

Terraforming, 2018, PRRB Publishing, ISBN-1790308100.

Martian Railroad, 2019, PRRB Publishing, ISBN-1794488243.

Exoplanets, 2019, PRRB Publishing, ISBN-1731385056.

Exploiting the Moon, 2019, PRRB Publishing, ISBN-1091057850.

RISC-V, an Open Source Solution for Space Flight Computers, 2019, PRRB Publishing, ISBN-1796434388.

Arm in Space, 2019, PRRB Publishing, ISBN-9781099789137.

Search for *Extraterrestrial Life*, 2019, PRRB Publishing, ISBN-978-1072072188.

Submarine Launched Ballistic Missiles, 2019, ISBN-978-1088954904.

Space Command, Military in Space, 2019, PRRB Publishing, ISBN-978-1693005398.

Robotic Exploration of the Icy moons of the Gas Giants,

ISBN- 979-8621431006.

History & Future of Cubesats, ISBN-978-1986536356.

Robotic Exploration of the Icy Moons of the Ice Giants, by Swarms of Cubesats, ISBN-979-8621431006.

Swarm Robotics, ISBN-979-8534505948.

Introduction to Electric Power Systems, ISBN-979-8519208727.

Powerships, Powerbarges, Floating Wind Farms: electricity when and where you need it, 2021, PRRB Publishing, ISBN-979-8716199477.

Centros de Control: Operaciones en Satélites del Estándar CubeSat (Spanish Edition), 2021, ISBN-979-8510113068.

The Artemis Missions, Return to the Moon, and on to Mars, 2021, ISBN-979-8490532361.

James Webb Space Telescope. A New Era in Astronomy, 2021, ISBN-979-8773857969.